Speaking
to the
Third
World

Speaking to the Third World

Essays on Democracy and Development

Peter L. Berger and Michael Novak

American Enterprise Institute for Public Policy Research
Washington, D.C.

Peter L. Berger is University Professor at Boston University and an adjunct scholar at AEI. His eleven books include *Pyramids of Sacrifice*, *The Heretical Imperative*, and *The War over the Family* (with Brigitte Berger). He is currently writing a book on the social and political theory of capitalism, *Capitalism and Society*. Michael Novak holds the George Frederick Jewett Chair at AEI and is the author of numerous books, including *The Spirit of Democratic Capitalism* and *Freedom With Justice*. He is a founding editor of *This World* and of *Catholicism in Crisis*, he has served as head of the U.S. delegation to the UN Human Rights Commission, and now serves on the Board for International Broadcasting, the private corporation governing Radio Free Europe and Radio Liberty.

Distributed by arrangement with

UPA, Inc.
4720 Boston Way
Lanham, MD 20706
3 Henrietta Street
London WC2E 8LU, England

Library of Congress Cataloging-in-Publication Data

Berger, Peter L.
    Speaking to the Third World.

    (AEI studies ; 425)
    1. Developing countries—Addresses, essays, lectures.
2. Democracy—Addresses, essays, lectures.   I. Novak,
Michael.   II. Title.   III. Series.
HC59.7.B388645   1985   338.9'009172'4   85-13329
ISBN 0-8447-3581-7 (alk. paper)
AEI Studies 425

Printed in the United States of America

Contents

FOREWORD *William J. Baroody, Jr.*

INTRODUCTION   1

SPEAKING TO THE THIRD WORLD *Peter L. Berger*   4

UNDERDEVELOPMENT REVISITED *Peter L. Berger*   21

DEMOCRACY AND HUMAN RIGHTS *Michael Novak*   31
    Introduction   31
    Human Rights and Institutions   34
    Utopian Revolution versus Realistic Revolution   38
    Confusions about Democracy   40
    Lessons for Catholic Social Thought   42
    Conclusion   44

DEMOCRACY AND DEVELOPMENT *Michael Novak*   45
    Toward a Theology of Democracy and Development   53
    Conclusion   58

Foreword

In the field of religion and economics, the themes of "democracy" and "development" are especially important today. For this reason, AEI's program in Religion, Philosophy, and Public Policy has returned to this subject in such publications as *Liberation South, Liberation North; Capitalism and Socialism: A Theological Inquiry;* and *The Corporation: A Theological Inquiry.* To this list, we now add the four useful essays collected here, in a way that strengthens each by conjunction with the others.

Peter L. Berger, author of the first two essays, is University Professor at Boston University and an Adjunct Scholar at AEI. His books include *Pyramids of Sacrifice, The Heretical Imperative,* and *The War over the Family* (with Brigitte Berger). He is currently writing a book on the social and political theory of capitalism, *Capitalism and Society.* Both of his essays herein reprinted first appeared in *Commentary.* Michael Novak, who holds the George Frederick Jewett chair at AEI, is the author of numerous books, including *The Spirit of Democratic Capitalism, Confession of a Catholic,* and most recently, *Freedom With Justice: Catholic Social Thought and Liberal Institutions.* Both of his articles are derived from lectures originally delivered in Chile, Mexico, and Korea; they first appeared in *Catholicism in Crisis.*

WILLIAM J. BAROODY, JR.
President,
American Enterprise Institute

Introduction

Michael Novak

The Revolution Is Moral or Not at All

We live in an age in which the entire world sees for the first time that the poverty of the poor is not necessary. Of the world's 160 or so nations, a substantial minority has made great strides toward virtually eliminating destitution. This is true not only among the so-called "advanced" societies but also among some of the more highly developed of the "less-developed" countries. Inevitably, though, "relative" poverty continues, and higher and higher standards are applied in defining it.

Some nations with few natural resources have made great strides in raising up the poor. That fact alone has given special poignancy to the universal cry for the elimination of poverty. The achievement of some gives hope to all the others. If nations with few material resources can achieve so much, why cannot those with abundant material resources?

Thus, much of the debate about the poor nations can no longer be couched solely in material terms. Increasingly, the experts see that it must also be couched in terms of morality, ethos, and culture. The systems of political economy of the world's many nations are not equally well designed to achieve either economic development (liberation from poverty) or political development (liberation from tyranny). The design of each system is crucial and is chiefly a moral matter. For embodied in the principles of internal social organization are social habits, the ethos of peoples, and quotidian institutions. "The revolution is moral or not at all," the young French philosopher-poet Charles Péguy once wrote. Moral questions about the design of systems are of the essence. Economists sometimes speak of such socially embodied human advantages, as well as of acquired technical skills and aptitudes, as "human capital."

Two generations ago, in his great five-volume *Lehrbuch der Nationalökonomie,* the great Jesuit and pioneering theologian of economics Heinrich Pesch stressed over and over again the essential role that the moral (even theological) life of a people plays in its economic de-

1

velopment. He wrote: "Morally advanced peoples will, no doubt, profit economically from the active, especially the social, virtues of their citizens and will be better prepared to endure physical evil and hard times."

That is why for Peter Berger and myself, in the four essays collected here, the worldwide discussion of "the development of peoples" (Pope Paul VI) is, inevitably, a moral discussion. It is an argument over the fundamental moral principles to be embodied in political economy. *Economic development has moral and cultural presuppositions.* Fundamental moral principles such as the dignity of every human person, the social nature of humankind, the freedoms of human association, and the like are at stake.

The intellectual elites of various parts of the underdeveloped world often share intellectual traditions quite different from those of the Anglo-American experience. One cannot simply assume that ideas that are part of our own intellectual patrimony in the United States have ever been heard, let alone soberly considered, by all participants in the international discussion. The bookstores surrounding the universities of many developing nations fairly teem with Marxist tracts in cheap editions, whereas the classics of Anglo-American life—from Adam Smith, Edmund Burke, and John Stuart Mill to *The Federalist,* Jefferson, Lincoln, and the multitudes of contemporary texts—are scarcely to be seen. The socialist intellectual networks practice propaganda and ideological penetration on a scale scarcely to be believed; one must see it with one's own eyes. In such circumstances, "dialogue" is scarcely in evidence; declamation is the prevailing mode. The nonsocialist side of the discussion (in all its immense variety and range) is seldom heard.

For this reason, it is important that the elites of the developing world have a chance not only to be listened to but also to be spoken to. It is important for North Americans, above all, not only to listen to, but also to speak to, the Third World. There must be dialogue, not monologue.

Such a dialogue must, of course, be conducted with civility, sensitivity, and reasoned discourse. I myself write these words just after returning from a week of vivid argumentation in three major cities in Brazil: Rio de Janeiro, Belo Horizonte, and Sao Paulo. I can testify first-hand that the main principles of Anglo-American democracy and capitalist development have, at least in some quarters, never been heard. They strike some listeners as (a phrase I heard more than once) "coming from another planet." American civilization errs seriously if it merely sends foreign aid, developmental assistance, investment, loans, technology transfers, multinational corporations, and bilateral assistance (whether public or private) *while not making clear the moral principles without which such material and technical assistance makes no human sense.* "The revolution is moral or not at all."

Peter L. Berger first addressed the subject of development, both socialist and capitalist, in a provocative volume, *Pyramids of Sacrifice* (1974). In recent years he has returned to the subject in a three-volume series he is now editing, as well as in the two articles from *Commentary* included in this collection. A world-renowned sociologist, Professor Berger is remarkable for his broad human sympathies, his capacity for intellectual detachment, and his sober respect for fact. His articles are pregnant with shrewd observation and good sense. I feel privileged to add my own reflections, from a somewhat more remote philosophical and theological point of view, to his own. These reflections were first formulated for lectures given in Santiago, Chile, where later they were republished in Spanish.

There can be no doubt that those of us privileged to live in free and prosperous societies have many weighty obligations with respect to the poor of the world. It is our task to listen, to observe, to reflect—and then to speak out clearly about those practical principles we think (rightly or wrongly) are most likely actually to help the poor of the world. Professor Berger and I offer our reflections, not as a final word, but as a dialogic word. We await eagerly the critique and the response of others, especially of those "liberation theologians" who, for one reason or another, disagree with us. Only so does genuine dialogue go forward, in the mutual and respectful search for those ideas that actually effect what they set forth: the liberation of the poor from both tyranny and poverty.

Speaking to the Third World

Peter L. Berger

"Third World." The very phrase by now evokes a multitude of images, positive as well as negative. Empirically, of course, the words bear little resemblance to reality—except, perhaps, at the United Nations, where the so-called Group of 77 does possess a real political form. But what, after all, do Brazil and Bangladesh have in common, or Singapore and the Seychelles, not to mention the oil-rich nations of the Gulf and the starvation-ridden countries of the Sahel? The so-called Third World includes countries of astronomically diverse economic, social, political, and cultural characteristics.

There are alternative terms. Within the United Nations, parlance has shifted from "underdeveloped countries" to "developing" to "less developed," each creating difficulties of its own. There is also the currently fashionable term "South," as in the "North/South dialogue" or "North/South global negotiations" urgently propagated by the Brandt Report and other voices for reform of the international system. This terminology, if nothing else, suffers from geographical absurdity. India is "South" and Australia "North," while the industrial societies of the Soviet bloc are in a never-never land left out of the "dialogue" altogether.

Political language is rarely an exercise in scientific logic, however, and chances are that we are stuck with the terms we have. The Third World, whatever else it may or may not be, is a rhetorical reality, and when Americans speak to the poorer nations of Asia, Africa, and Latin America (and even to some of the less poor nations in those regions), they are indeed addressing the Third World.

The phrase itself originated in the early 1950s, and was solemnly proclaimed as a reality at the Bandung conference of 1955, when a number of "nonaligned" countries (including Sukarno's Indonesia, Nehru's India, and Tito's Yugoslavia) asserted their right to pursue a path independent of the two superpower blocs. But already more was implied with respect to the American and Soviet systems than simple nonalignment. There was also the notion of a "third way" of development, different from the allegedly flawed models of American-style capitalism and Soviet-style Communism. Just what that third way might be was never spelled out with much precision. Presumably it was more socialist than the American model and more democratic than the Soviet one—some sort of social democracy, yet not simply a copy of Western models, rather an indigenous construction doing justice to the cultural traditions of the countries first gathered at Bandung.

These implications have remained in place. Although the quarter-century that has elapsed since Bandung has not produced a sharper definition of the development "model" to which all of the countries concerned (by now well over one hundred) might jointly adhere, this vagueness has not prevented the emergence of something that could accurately be called a Third World ideology. Nor has it prevented powerful emotional associations with the phrase "Third World," not only in the countries deemed to belong to that world but in Western countries as well.

In the Western mind, the phrase evokes eschatological themes dating all the way back to Joachim of Flora's Third Age and to the dream of a Third Rome (leaving aside the obscene parody of these themes in the myth of the Third Reich propagated by the Nazis, who also took that phrase from much earlier sources). For leftists there is the additional association with the threefold Hegelian dialectic, the third moment of which, the "synthesis," is to solve redemptively the contradictions of the preceding thesis and antithesis (in this case, presumably, the contradictions between capitalism and Communism).

In recent decades, and particularly since the 1960s, the Third World has served as a gigantic Rorschach card onto which Westerners have projected their fantasies, their fears, and their hopes of salvation. Academic experts in "nation-building," Peace Corps volunteers, and would-be revolutionaries have flocked to this or that Third World country in search of a suitable laboratory for their particular projects of designed social change. In the 1960s and 1970s, the New Left, eager to find a Marxist experiment free of the acknowledged flaws of the Soviet model, enthroned one Third World country after another as the locale of humane socialism: Cuba, China, North Vietnam, more esoterically Tanzania or Mozambique, for a brief moment of glory Allende's Chile, more recently Nicaragua. The counterculture evinced a generalized interest in the Third World as the place where simpler, healthier, and spiritually more profound ways of life were to be found—for years young people in peasant clothes, looking for the peasants with whom to affiliate, commuted haplessly between Kabul and Katmandu or meditated on the beaches of Goa, prey to every guru on the make. The same Third World of the imagination continues to haunt a miscellany of counter-modern movements in Western countries—such radical offshoots of environmentalism as anti-nuclear activists, zero-growth enthusiasts, advocates of solar energy and holistic healing, propagandists of "alternate technology" and Tantric meditation.

Needless to say, these people have contributed little if anything to the countries to which they have come as political pilgrims (to use Paul Hollander's apt term), while at home their main contribution has been to legitimate various tyrannies. Still, only a relatively small group of people in America and other Western countries have utilized the Third World in this manner. (In Western Europe the phenomenon still appears to be on the rise, while in America it has been declining.)

Not surprisingly, there has also been a counterimage of the Third World—an image of hopelessly corrupt, incompetent, and oppressive regimes, opposed to American purposes and ideals. In this conception of the Third World, instead of noble revolutionaries and wholesome peasants, we get predatory dictators; the only way to deal with such regimes is to ignore them or tell them off.

As an overall stance toward the Third World, an attitude of contempt and hostility is no better than an attitude of awed and guilt-ridden admiration. If nothing else, the aforementioned diversity of the Third World should preclude such one-sided responses. The Third World is not an arena for our utopianisms; neither is it a zone in which to locate our sundry demonologies.

Just because so much nonsense has been spouted about the Third World, it is useful to step back and try to gain some perspective on a phenomenon which is, at bottom, nothing less than the entry onto the stage of history of vast masses of people who until now have lived in a situation that can be accurately described as pre-historical.

Immense anguish and pain, physical as well as moral, have been associated with the entry of these people into the common history of our age. There is a timeless dignity to the forms of human existence provided by tribe, village, and other traditional structures, and the disturbance of these life-forms by the turbulent forces of modernity has hardly been an unambiguous boon. Yet many if not most of the images of anguish turn out, upon closer scrutiny, to be superimposed upon images of hope.

Take one of the most common negative images of Third World development—the overcrowded slums of the enormous urban agglomerations of Asia, Africa, and Latin America, symbolized by the names of Calcutta, Lagos, Mexico City, and all those other cities that impress one as gigantic explosions, human volcanoes in cataclysmic eruption. It is easy to contrast the turbulence and undeniable misery of these places with the supposed tranquility and relative content-ment of the villages from which most of their inhabitants have only just arrived. But there is another side to the picture. The overwhelm-ing majority of the people in these urban agglomerations have come to the cities voluntarily. What is more, they have come knowing full well what to expect: Third World peasants are no less rational than Western intellectuals in making important decisions for themselves and their children, and the networks of clan and caste insure that highly reliable information is fed back to home villages. Why do they keep coming? The answer is very simple: because they have reason to believe that their chances of a better life are greater in the cities than at home.

Thus the vast migrations of the Third World are not mindless movements of dehumanized and desperate masses (as depicted, for example, in the apocalyptic novel *The Camp of the Saints* by the French writer Jean Raspail). Rather, they represent the quest of countless individuals and families for a life of greater dignity and decency. To be sure, that quest is often frustrated. Many times over, however, it is realized. And precisely in places like Calcutta one is impressed by the vitality, courage, and resourcefulness of people who, all at once, are given hope of a better life.

If one asks *why* so much of the Third World is so crowded, the reason is not high birth rates; it is the dramatic lowering of death rates, and particularly of the rates of infant mortality. This change begins to take place even at very rudimentary levels of economic development, with the introduction of quite modest improvements in nutrition and hygiene. The human consequence of this change is extraordinarily simple: whereas, previously, most children died, now more and more children survive. In this there is joy and hope, and it is precisely these emotions that fuel the energy with which much of the Third World seems to overflow. No amount of skepticism about the blessings of modernity can nullify the human and moral progress which this change signifies.

It cannot surprise us that politics in these cataclysmic circum-stances should be volatile, often violent, often irrational. But the poli-tics of the putatively more developed West have not exactly been a model of order and rationality in this century. (An observer from Zaire, once a colony of Belgium, noted mordantly that the irrational conflicts between the French and the Flemish in that country, which have brought about the irremediable destruction of the ancient uni-versity of Louvain, one of the historic centers of Western learning, clearly demonstrate that Belgium is not yet ripe for self-government.)

It is all too easy to denigrate the nascent nationalisms of the Third World, to ridicule such practices as the investment of scarce capital in the "empty symbolism" of, for example, a national airline. But this self-affirmation of people who only yesterday, so far as the rest of the world was concerned, were silent, must also be part of our understanding of the Third World. It is something to be affirmed, even celebrated.

If the ideology of the Third World consisted only in proclaiming these realities, we should have no serious difficulty with it. Even if that ideology insisted that it was our obligation, humanly and morally, to help, we should assent. The eradication of starvation and of degrading misery is a moral imperative for states and for the international community, as well as for concerned citizens and nongovernmental groups in rich countries. Unfortunately, Third World ideology has gone considerably beyond such propositions, and it is not possible, either intellectually or morally, to assent to it as a whole.

Not that the Third World is an ideological monolith. Just as it is diverse in its economic, social, and political realities, so is it diverse ideologically. It contains explicitly Marxist states and explicitly anti-Marxist ones, states (notably in the Muslim world) that profess to be governed by religious tradition and emphatically secular states. If one speaks of a Third World ideology, then, one is referring to an "ideal type." This does not mean that the type has no relation to reality. It does. The reality surfaces most visibly within the United Nations system on those occasions when Third World countries agree on a common position (which happens quite frequently).

To be sure, even within the United Nations different states proclaim this ideology with different nuances and varying forcefulness. Singapore does not speak like India, Senegal says different things from Ethiopia, Brazil from Mexico. But one interesting and unifying aspect should be noted: the construction that one may call the Third World ideology is, broadly speaking, leftist—indeed, in important intellectual respects it depends on elements of Marxist theory—and it is given lip service by states that are anything but leftist in their domestic arrangements. If one asks why that should be, the answer, one must surmise, is that these states expect to gain, politically or economically, from a rhetorical adherence to positions which happen to contradict their own internal strategies. This is distressing—but also hopeful, for it shows the fragile basis of the Third World consensus and provides openings for dissenting points of view.

With these qualifications, it is possible to point to a series of propositions as the common core of the Third World ideology:

- Development is not just a matter of economic growth. Rather, one can only regard as development those processes of change in which the dynamism of economic growth is harnessed to transcendent social purposes—to the progressive rescue from degrading poverty of masses of people and to a more egalitarian distribution of the benefits of growth.

• The causes of Third World poverty must be sought primarily outside the Third World itself—historically in the depredations of colonialism and imperialism, today in the consequences of an unjust international economic system which is heavily weighted in favor of the rich countries of the West (or "North") against the poor countries of the Third World (or "South").

• The West owes "compensation" or "reparations" to the Third World for past acts of exploitation. Also, the West owes the Third World a redress of the unjust international economic system through a variety of juridical, political, and economic measures. This, in the long run, will be of benefit to all countries, as it will result in a more stable world order.

• The establishment of a just international system is a prerequisite for all aspects of development, not only economic but political and human as well. For that reason economic and social rights must be accorded parity with civil and political rights within the general conception of human rights espoused by the international community.

These propositions constitute an intellectual and moral whole. That is, they are based on a set of presuppositions about the nature of the world and they also put this view of the world into a moral context, a view of what the world *ought* to be. Moreover, this ideology, culled from a variety of sources (most of them, incidentally, of Western provenance), is not an abstract intellectual enterprise. Rather it is a political instrument, used to legitimate specific objectives. Thus the broad acceptance of this ideology by Third World governments has gone hand in hand with various political initiatives, almost all of them within the United Nations system.

These initiatives have not only been aimed at securing favorable treatment for Third World countries in terms of trade and aid, but have also sought to enshrine some of the features of Third World ideology in international law. In 1974, the United Nations General Assembly adopted a Charter of Economic Rights and Duties of States. This was meant to forge into a juridical instrument the calls for a New International Economic Order, which, first issued by Mexico in the early 1970s, had increasingly become a rallying point for the Group of 77.

This thrust to establish a legal foundation for Third World demands continues today in efforts to change the structure of international monetary institutions, to set in motion a multilateral process of "global negotiations," and to recognize the "right to development" as a fundamental human right (individual as well as collective). A French commentator on this process, Alain Pellet, has aptly described it as one in which "recommendations" are progressively transformed into "obligations." The United States and other Western states have continually resisted these efforts to make the United Nations into a quasi-legislative body on behalf of Third World concerns, but the Group of 77 has been able to override most of the resistance within the United Nations system. (The real world outside the United Nations enclaves of New York, Geneva, and Vienna has been less tractable.)

This is not the place to discuss the far-reaching juridical problems relevant to the Third World initiatives. Nor is it the place to go into the economic and political questions that are currently on the agenda of "global negotiations"—terms of trade, aid levels, control over natural resources, regulation of transnational corporations, and the like. What I should like to do here is to formulate a possible American response to the main themes of Third World ideology.

It is clear that, with one or two exceptions, such a response must be mainly negative—as, indeed, it has been when American spokesmen have confronted elements of the ideology in the United Nations. Maintaining such a negative stance is not comfortable—not for the individuals who must appear in international forums where the emotional temperature is often very high, and not for a people that historically has an idealistic image of itself and a strong psychological need to be liked.

Thus one question that must be considered immediately is whether Americans are wise to put themselves into such a negative position. It is a question often raised by Europeans. After all, they say, what is at issue here is mainly words; the United Nations itself is largely a word factory, and the words mean very little; for public-relations reasons, since nothing substantive is being given away, why not give "them" the words they want?

The suggestion is attractive (perhaps especially so to anyone who has been forced to listen to the endless rhetoric of international meetings at which Third World spokesmen angrily present their views). Yet it must be firmly rejected, and for two reasons, one political and one moral. Politically, it is an error (if you will, a vulgar Marxist error) to believe that words mean nothing. Words embody ideas, and ideas have real consequences, in the long run if not immediately. Morally, the attitude of giving "them" words rather than substance is patronizing, even an expression of contempt (in the case of some Europeans, one suspects a continuity here with attitudes of the not-sodistant colonial past). Whatever we may think about their views on some matters, Americans must confront their Third World interlocutors as equals. It is to equals that one is free to say "no." And it is "no" that we must often say.

Often, but not always. To the proposition that development is not the same as economic growth, we can indeed assent. Demurring from the overemphasis on equality, we can also assent to a definition of development that includes greater access to a decent life and institutions for the protection of the human rights of everyone in society.

But we must dissent from the fundamental idea of economic relations that underlies the Third World ideology. This is a vast elaboration of Proudhon's dictum that property is theft. Economic relations are seen here as a zero-sum game. The gain of one is necessarily the loss of another. Wealth is acquired at the expense of the poor. Resources are owned by one and taken away by the other. To be sure, there are such cases, and they can be appropriately characterized as exploitation, but they are the exception rather than the rule. More to the point, this exploitation "model" does not fit the relations between the Third World and the advanced societies of the West either in the past or today.

The thesis that colonialism and imperialism impoverished and hampered the development of Third World societies is highly questionable, to say the least. As P. T. Bauer has pointed out repeatedly, the poorest countries tend to be those whose economic relations with the West have been minimal, while many ex-colonies have done very well indeed. There is no way in which the affluence of a long list of Western countries, including the United States, can be causally explained by colonial exploitation. As for the great colonial powers themselves, such as Britain and France, historians will argue for a long time whether they in fact got more from their colonies than they put into them.

It is also very questionable whether the contemporary international system can be described as exploitative in the sense that "Northern" wealth is extracted from "Southern" poverty. With the exception of some natural resources, among which oil is paramount, the economies of the "North" are quite independent of the "South." Indeed, that is precisely the problem for Third World economies, which, in order to develop, must seek to enter the "rich" system under favorable conditions. This is a very real problem and a difficult one, and one with a moral dimension. Recognition of that dimension, however, stems from our common humanity and from the solidarity between nations. It is not something that can be optimistically pro-

11

claimed in various international instruments; it cannot stem from distorted history, bad law, or pathological guilt feelings.

The demand for "compensation" or "reparations" is thus spurious—historically, juridically, and morally. It is also absurd: one need only ask whether it recognizes any statute of limitations or how the putative debtors are to be defined. Can Hungary demand compensation from Mongolia for the depredations of Genghis Khan? Are black Americans to sue the states of West Africa for the collusion of past political authorities with the slave trade?

There is an even more serious distortion of economic reality in Third World ideology. That is the emphasis on external rather than internal "obstacles to development." These external obstacles are recurrently invoked in what has by now become a litany of exorcism— "imperialism, colonialism, neocolonialism, racism, *apartheid*," to which catalogue, for good measure, "Zionism" is occasionally added. The litany is mostly malicious nonsense.

Let it be stipulated that there are, in fact, situations where external forces serve to impede the development of a country. In these situations the character and strength of such forces must be assessed, and the country in question is fully entitled to seek relief by whatever means. I would contend, though, that such situations are quite rare— except in the massive case of Soviet imperialism, which, for reasons that are patently political, is hardly ever mentioned in this context.

The most frequent "obstacles to development" are internal to the societies in quest of development. Among such obstacles are economic systems that stultify growth and impede productivity; political corruption; oppression of people to the point where they cease to be economically active; persecution of economically productive minorities (such as the Asians in eastern Africa and the Chinese in southeast Asia); and, in some cases, indigenous social patterns and cultural values that are not conducive to economic activity. The fixation on external villains is a convenient stratagem for Third World elites who are either unable or unwilling to face up to internal obstacles. There is no reason, however, why we should fortify them in this evasion.

One may note here as well the tendency of Third World spokesmen and their sympathizers in the West to stress the allegedly growing gap between rich and poor nations and the deteriorating condition of the Third World as a whole. Both propositions are dubious. It is not at all clear that the gap is broadening, especially in recent years when Western economies have faced serious difficulties, many of them caused by the astronomical rise in energy costs (OPEC is virtually never mentioned in Third World pronouncements as a cause of poverty in these countries—roughly for the same reasons Soviet imperialism is not mentioned). And while the condition of some countries has deteriorated, there have also been phenomenal success stories in the Third World, such as those of South Korea, Taiwan, and some of the ASEAN states.

What with all the emphasis on juridical instruments and agreements between states, one gets the impression that many Third World representatives look upon development as something to be wrested from others—namely, the industrialized countries of the West, or rather their governments. It is to be development by fiat, following upon a political struggle in which concessions are won by moral suasion or by pressures of various sorts.

This strange view is perhaps encouraged by the unreality of the United Nations, in which words appear to take on a life of their own, and by the simple fact that the "North-South dialogue" is mainly conducted by government officials who tend to hold an exaggerated idea of the importance of political institutions.

All of this, however, obfuscates the fact that development, in any meaning of the term, cannot be the result of juridical and political arrangements between states (though such arrangements can be useful in particular instances). Development is the result of the sustained economic activity of large numbers of people, the result of effort, hard work, and ingenuity. It cannot be wrested from someone else, like a chunk of valuable matter. Indeed, such a view masks a paternalism of its own, for if development is something that can be wrested from us in the West, then it is we who grant it. This stands in curious contradiction to the oft-repeated Third World principles of self-reliance and freedom from dependency. Whatever development may mean, it should not mean the establishment of an international welfare system.

The bias in Third World statements about development derives from the fact that many Third World regimes follow some variety of socialism both in theory and practice, while many others, if not socialist, are heavily statist in their economic system. Although a detailed discussion of socialist models of development would take many pages, suffice it to say that among the socialist regimes of the Third World there is not a single success story—defining success not in "our" terms but, precisely, in the Third World terms of victory over the more wretched forms of poverty and a reasonable degree of egalitarian distribution. The typical record of Third World socialism is one of economic stagnation, often perpetuating abject poverty if not outright starvation; the species of egalitarianism that prevails among the "masses" is one of an equality among serfs, lorded over by a privileged elite of party bureaucrats and managers. Shmuel Eisenstadt has

13

called this system "neo-patrimonialism"; Pierre Bourdieu's term, "socialo-feudalism," is also apt. The vast panorama of "different paths to development" in the contemporary world only reinforces the conclusion that socialism is incapable of producing in terms of its own promises.

In non-socialist cases, too, it is quite clear that the state as such is not the bearer of development. At best, states can institute policies that *leave room* for the real agents of development—enterprising individuals, families, clans, *compadre* groupings, and other traditional units, and more modern associations such as cooperatives or credit unions.

The moral aspect of this ought to be stressed. A heavy moral responsibility rests on those who impose unproductive and inefficient economic arrangements on developing societies, doubly so when these arrangements are adhered to in the face of hunger, disease, and degrading poverty. It is obscenely inappropriate when the very people who propagate this criminal waste of human and material resources claim to be or to represent the "party of compassion."

Official United Nations declarations and position papers are reassuringly clear on one point: economic, social, and cultural rights are to be thought of as an indivisible whole with civil and political rights, and neither set of rights is to be given priority over the other. This would seem to be official Secretariat doctrine and, on the face of it, would preclude the notion that civil and political rights can be set aside until certain economic and social goals have been achieved (in the manner of both Marxist and other "development dictatorships"). Unfortunately, Third World spokesmen are not always so clear. There is often the suggestion that civil and political rights are devoid of real meaning unless or until economic and social rights have been secured. Worse, the securing of the latter set of rights is now often identified with the establishment of the New International Economic Order, an eschatological event comparable to the final passage to Communism in Marxist thought. This facet of Third World ideology, which offers a pretext for legitimizing sundry violations of human rights in the unredeemed present, is but another version of a gambit favored by many tyrants of our age.

There is one last element of Third World ideology to which we may give at least qualified assent—that is the proposition that Third World development is in the long-term interest of the industrial societies of the West. This proposition is often advanced on economic grounds (as in the Brandt Report), reflecting a Keynesian view of economics that many in the West will not find persuasive today; if Keynesian economics has not worked very well within societies, one may be skeptical about its working between societies. On political grounds, however, there is much to be said for the proposition. A permanently impoverished, politically turbulent Third World cannot be in the interest of the industrial democracies of the West, and steps to forestall such a situation can be seen as expressions of self-interest.

It is appropriate to appeal to people to do things out of self-interest; it is difficult to do so while at the same time denouncing them. In their stance toward the West, Third World spokesmen will have to choose between statesmanship and evangelism; both cannot be plausibly exercised simultaneously. Of the two, statesmanship would appear to be the more promising course.

Given the adversary posture of Third World ideology vis-à-vis the United States, it is inevitable that Americans will have to adopt a critical stance. At the same time, Americans must have the confidence to present a positive model of development that is properly their own—to present, that is, an American ideology of development. Americans had such confidence before the recent period of national self-criticism, and some of it, let it be conceded, was overconfidence. The idea that the American experience could be directly transplanted to the Third World and emulated there in all its details was dubious even in the 1950s. It is both intellectually dubious and politically ineffective now. What we must rather do (and this is by no means an easy task) is to isolate certain key elements of the American experience which are not necessarily dependent on the peculiar historical and cultural features of our society, and define the manner and degree to which they can be transplanted to different societies.

Two such elements stand out: democracy and capitalism. At the heart of any American ideology of development must lie the concept of democratic capitalism, to use the felicitous phrase which Michael Novak has introduced. Specifically, what needs to be shown is that the human benefits associated with the democratic ideal are linked empirically (and perhaps linked necessarily) with societal arrangements that, minimally, leave important sectors of the economy to the free operation of market forces.

We do not, at this point, possess a comprehensive theory of capitalism, but one thing we know is the empirical correlation between capitalism and political liberty (as well as the correlation between political liberty and the whole gamut of human rights). That correlation can be stated with great precision: every democracy in the contemporary world has a capitalist economy; no society with a socialist economy is democratic. The fact that a sizable number of countries, all now in the Third World, are capitalist *and* non-democratic does not negate the correlation between democracy and

15

capitalism, which can be theoretically explicated in terms of the brakes on state power that a private sector *tends* to produce.

Another thing about which we know a good deal is the relationship between economic systems and success in the achievement of development goals. As I noted above, there is not a single socialist success story; all the success stories have occurred in countries with capitalist systems. We do not as yet know enough about the reasons for the failure of some capitalist systems. Obviously all societal decisions entail risks; there are no guarantees. But if the goal is *both* development *and* institutions protecting liberty and human rights, capitalist economic arrangements are the better bet.

This does not mean that Americans should engage in a great crusade to make the world safe for democratic capitalism. We do not have the power to do this and, even if we had, we should respect those who choose other directions (assuming, which is rare, that they choose freely). But this need not prevent us from speaking openly and without embarrassment about the realities that we perceive, even if doing so puts us in a minority position in most international forums and among intellectuals in most countries. The socialist vision has been *the* grand fantasy of our age; amid all the celebrations of illusion and wishful thinking, it may be the mission of America to represent the "reality principle."

The practical implication is that American advice and assistance on development (by government as well as by non-governmental bodies) should emphasize the private sector and private entrepreneurship wherever possible. Such an emphasis by no means implies focusing on the large transnational corporations (though the demonological view of these institutions should be repudiated). Rather, the focus should be on indigenous enterprise, much of it small and precarious. Most important of all, the focus should be on the privately owned and operated family farm, which virtually everywhere has been the agent of successful agrarian development.

There are a good many Third World societies in which such an emphasis on the private sector is not practicable. But even in socialist or heavily statist societies, it is an illusion that economic activity can be totally controlled from the political command posts. Development is invariably the fruit of individual and small-group effort, and Americans should reiterate this elementary fact over and over again in the face of the self-aggrandizing delusions of bureaucrats and intellectuals.

It must also be a part of the American position on development that democracy, with its panoply of protections for individual rights, is not a luxury of the rich. On the contrary, it is the poor who need democracy much more urgently than the rich. In most places, certainly in most places in the Third World, the rich manage to protect their interests. It is the poor who need the institutional protections of liberty the most—protection against the arbitrary powers of local police, against employers who would deny them the right to organize, against those who would prevent a journalist from writing about conditions of poverty, and so on.

The proposition that democracy is a luxury of rich *countries* is also false. Democracy and development may not be invariably linked phenomena, but most countries in which democracy has been suppressed in the name of development have not attained their development goals, either. On the other hand, in authoritarian regimes, as development gains the pressures for democracy increase.

In the development literature as well as in the rhetoric of Third World spokesmen there is much talk about "participation"—the notion that people should be the subjects rather than the objects of development strategies. But participation outside the framework of a democratic polity is invariably questionable. "Mobilization" is not participation; it is usually the opposite, the regimentation of people in the service of projects to which they did not agree and over which they have no control. And even in democratic or near-democratic situations the meaning of the term is not always clear. Participation means little unless the values and indigenous institutions of the people engaged in development efforts are respected by the authorities. It is very important to stress that, in most Third World countries, these are *traditional* values and *traditional* institutions. Americans should always insist on the literal meaning of the term "participation" and debunk relentlessly situations in which the term is used to camouflage the imposition of social-engineering designs on people who were never asked. In other words, participation means that people have real choices and real influence, or it means nothing at all.

One of the most intractable problems of modern life concerns the fate of those institutions ("mediating structures" in sociological parlance) which stand between the individual and the macro-structures of the state. These are the institutions that provide meaning and identity to individuals. Paramount among them in all societies are the family and the religious community. In Third World societies other groupings of a traditional character have to be added—clan, tribe, caste, village, ethnic and regional subcultures. Superimposed on these, and existing often in a symbiotic relation to them, are a variety of local economic, social, and political associations of modern provenance.

A good case can be made that development strategies which

ignore or run roughshod over such mediating structures are unlikely to succeed. This case should be made strongly by Americans, as against the totalitarian tendencies in much thinking about the Third World. But the case should be related to the argument for democratic capitalism. Capitalism "leaves room" for mediating structures, while socialist development models almost always try to suppress, regiment, or (perhaps worst of all) "mobilize" them. Indeed, this tendency is causally related to the failures of socialist development; the record is particularly clear in the area of agriculture. What we now know about the fiasco of Maoist policies in China may serve as the *exemplum horribile* of such strategies.

Already in the 1950s the idea was prevalent that traditional values and institutions were "obstacles to development." But development strategies which defy tradition at all points run into great peril. Iran offers an important example. A counter-example is Japan, where, apparently to date, the society has successfully modernized while leaving traditional values and institutions intact over large areas of life. Similarly successful "creative schizophrenia" seems to be a factor in the development of Asian societies with a strong foundation in Confucian or neo-Confucian morality. Recent events in India are also instructive in this regard. Hinduism, more than any other traditional culture, has been characterized by development analysts as an "obstacle"; in the 1960s and 1970s India was always compared unfavorably with China. We now know, beyond a shadow of a doubt, the dismal reality of China's Maoist experiment. In India, in the meantime, there has taken place what may yet come to be seen as an agricultural miracle. The causes of this, as far as one can tell, have been a combination of technological innovation (the "Green Revolution") and imaginative government policies on credit and technical assistance to small farmers. It did *not* involve an attack on traditional Hindu values and social patterns. On the contrary, development has taken place within the traditional forms of Hindu village life.

Once again, Americans should speak for a view of modernity which does not regard traditional ways of life as something to be despised and discarded. And once again, the case should be made that for such purposes democratic capitalism provides the model.

The individuals who purport to speak in the name of the Third World are, typically, unelected and unrepresentative of anything but the tiny group that happens to hold state power at a particular moment. Even when they do represent elected governments, they typically belong to a very small elite with Western education and an international outlook. Most of them have as little knowledge of or contact with "the masses" of their own people as a Harvard professor purporting to represent "the masses" of America (happily, few Harvard professors make such a claim). We should not disguise our awareness of this fact. In addressing the Third World, we may often have to try and speak to people over the heads of their governments. We cannot do this everywhere with equal facility, but in many places we have the capacity if we have the will.

It has often been said that the United States is a conservative or counterrevolutionary power in the contemporary world. There is truth in this—*if* one looks at the world in purely political terms. American foreign policy has indeed been dominated by the desire to stabilize, while the other superpower has aimed to destabilize. But if one looks at the world in economic, social, and cultural terms, nothing could be farther from the truth. The Soviet Union represents economic stagnation, social conservatism, and cultural sterility. By contrast, the Western world, and the United States above all, brims over with economic, social, and cultural vitality. Whether one considers technological innovation, industrial and agricultural productivity, or the vast array of social and cultural experiments, it is America that is in the lead.

One can ascribe this vitality to a number of factors, but at the core of it is, precisely, the gigantic transforming power of democratic capitalism, that power which Joseph Schumpeter once called "creative destruction." Put simply: the only real revolution going on in the world today is that of democratic capitalism. Its adversaries represent counterrevolution and reaction.

The most important evidence for this elementary fact is the irresistible attraction of American culture—the culture *par excellence* of democratic capitalism—even in, indeed especially in, countries where anti-Americanism dominates political rhetoric. From the realm of ideas to the trivia of everyday living, from high culture to the least appetizing pop fashions, and across the entire range of material and non-material furnishings of what is considered a desirable "life style" (itself a deeply revealing term, of American origin), it is the symbols and the substance of American civilization that are sweeping the world. There seems to be no letup in this process, and no viable competitors have appeared on the scene. What is more, this revolutionary culture has the unique ability to thrive under conditions that foster freedom and that allow expression to a plurality of values, including many of the values of tradition.

Just as it is preposterous that the international Left, with its miserable and misery-creating record, still arrogates to itself the status of the "party of compassion," so it is preposterous that it pretends to be the party of revolution. In creating an American mode of address to the Third World, we should remind ourselves that we represent the only revolution in the world today that can credibly promise economic development, political liberty, and respect for the dignity of human beings in their infinite variety.

Underdevelopment Revisited

Peter L. Berger

The poverty in which large numbers of human beings live has been a stubborn and morally troubling reality for a long time. The terminology describing this reality has often changed, however. During the hopeful years of decolonization in the aftermath of World War II, "backwardness" (a term suggesting mental retardation) gave way to "underdevelopment" (implying a merely physical lag). This "underdevelopment" was to be cured by "development," in turn identified with "growth" (as a child catches up with an adult). The manifesto of this period was Walt W. Rostow's *The Stages of Economic Growth*, first published in 1960, and reminiscent of Jean Piaget's child psychology in its self-confident prescription of how a country develops from "take-off" to "maturity."

Then came the late 1960s and early 1970s, when this entire way of looking at the poorer portions of the globe was radically debunked, both in the "underdeveloped" countries themselves and in influential academic sectors of the West. Not only did the "children" throw the book at their "teachers," but many teachers recanted their earlier pedagogic doctrine. The quasi-mythological phrase "Third World" came into vogue, while the bureaucratic agencies concerned with the poorer regions fell back either on the relatively optimistic term "developing countries" or on the seemingly neutral term, "less developed countries" (with its official acronym, LDCs).

In the last few years, as the revolutionary redemptions of the "Third World" have proved ever more disappointing, the favored term has become "South," as in "North/South dialogue." "South" suggests sunshine, perhaps even natural abundance, but also languid siestas in the heat of the day. The ambiguity is telling.

Changes in terminology sometimes reflect advances in knowledge; sometimes they are covers for ignorance. Which is the case here? How much have we really learned about the world's poverty and the remedies for it?

If one is in the habit of writing books, these books can sometimes serve as convenient landmarks to measure both advances in learning and perduring ignorance. It is now almost exactly ten years since the publication of my *Pyramids of Sacrifice*, which was a tentative summing-up of what I had learned about "development" since becoming involved in the topic a few years earlier. As it happens, this book (somewhat to my surprise) is still being read; more importantly, it reflects a particular phase in the intellectual and political debate over the issue of poverty and development. For this reason a look at what I said in 1974 may be a useful exercise.

I wrote *Pyramids of Sacrifice* in response to two powerful experiences. One was my first contact with Third World poverty, which shocked me morally as well as emotionally. The other was the eruption in American academia of a neo-Marxist rhetoric, which purported to understand the causes of Third World poverty and which also claimed to know the remedies. I was never convinced by this rhetoric, but I wanted to be fair to it. More than anything else, I wanted to explore, with moral engagement and skeptical rationality, an area which at that time was suffused with violent emotions and blatantly irrational opinions.

The book argued that both capitalism and socialism had generated myths that had to be debunked—the capitalist myth of growth, which mistook an increase in GNP for improvement in the condition of the poor, and the socialist myth of revolution, which provided an alibi for tyranny. In the service of demythologizing these ideas, the book advocated an open, non-doctrinaire approach; neither capitalism nor socialism, it argued, offered a panacea. Each country would have to think through, in pragmatic terms, what its most promising development strategy should be. As far as moral criteria were concerned, such a pragmatic assessment should be guided, I thought, by two calculi—a "calculus of pain," by which I meant the avoidance of human suffering, and a "calculus of meaning," which I defined as respect for the values of the putative beneficiaries of development policies.

A centerpiece of the book was a comparison of Brazil and China, important respectively as the largest capitalist and the largest socialist case. I had traveled extensively in Brazil just before writing *Pyramids;* although I had not been to China, I had read voraciously about it. I concluded that both "models" should be rejected—curiously, for the same reason. Both were willing to sacrifice a generation for an allegedly certain goal of development, Brazil through the adoption of economic policies that condoned widespread and bitter misery as the short-run price for long-run prosperity, China through terror and totalitarianism. Neither the Brazilian technocrats nor the Chinese ideologists, I wrote, could be certain about the eventual outcome of their policies. This being so, they lost any moral warrant for the sacrifices they were imposing on their peoples.

Yet neither case, the book suggested, exhausted the possibilities of the capitalist or socialist development models. Capitalism need not be practiced as brutally as in Brazil, and there could be a more humane socialism than that of Maoist China. In this connection, I said some nice things about Peru (then under Velasco's Left-leaning regime) and Tanzania; I had been briefly in both places and had been favorably impressed.

A number of readers of *Pyramids of Sacrifice* were misled by my wish to be fair to the Left (which, practically, meant that I desired to go on talking with most of my colleagues). They read the book as advocating democratic socialism. That had not been my intention at all. What did come through, however, was some vague notion of a "third way," perhaps some sort of a so-called mixed model. I had no clear conception of what this might look like; I was unsure of much, and I admitted it. I did feel sure of two things, however: that people should not be allowed to starve if the means to feed them were at hand, and that people should not be subjected to totalitarian terror under any circumstances.

Obviously, *Pyramids of Sacrifice* is today obsolete, because of the changes that have taken place in the world (more of this below). But looking back on it now, I am struck as well by the changes that have occurred in my own perspective. Not to put too fine a point on it, I am much less evenhanded today in my assessment of capitalist and socialist development models: I have become much more emphatically pro-capitalist. Some part of the shift I have undergone is undoubtedly due to personal experience. In 1974, except for one foray into Africa, my acquaintance with the Third World was limited to Latin America; inevitably, this made for a very specific bias. In 1977, however, I had my first experience of East Asia and since then my attention has turned very strongly to that region. East Asia is inconvenient territory for those who want to be evenhanded as between capitalist and socialist development models. Specifically, the capitalist "success stories" of East Asia and the lessons they hold must be confronted by any reflective person with a concern for world poverty.

To speak of success stories implies a definition of success. And here I would today insist that, minimally, there are three criteria to be applied.

First, successful development presupposes sustained and self-generating economic growth. To that extent, at least, Rostow and the other enthusiasts of the 1950s were perfectly right, while the late fantasists of zero growth were perfectly wrong. We have a pretty clear idea of what a zero-growth world would look like. It would either freeze the existing inequities between rich and poor, or it would see a violent struggle to divide up a pie that is no longer growing. Neither scenario holds out the slightest promise for such values as human rights or democracy. The existing inequities would have to be brutally defended or brutally altered. I daresay that this root insight of political economy is by now widely recognized, even on the Left (except, perhaps, among the remaining holdouts of romantic environmentalism).

Secondly, successful development means the large-scale and sustained movement of people from a condition of degrading poverty to a minimally decent standard of living. In insisting on this point, I continue to give credence to the critique (mostly from the Left) of the earlier development theories, which tended to see economic growth as a synonym for development rather than as its precondition. On that point, the critics were right: the most impressive growth rates can cover up massively inequitable distribution of the benefits of growth; there can be growth without development, and there can even be what André Gunder Frank has called "the development of underdevelopment." Brazil in the early 1970s was a striking example of this—staggering economic growth, so maldistributed that abject misery (measured by hunger, infant mortality, low life expectancy, and the like) not only continued unabated but, in parts of Brazil, worsened.

I would even go a step farther in conceding a point to the Left. The advocates of liberation theology have contributed a phrase, "the preferential option for the poor," which sounds like a bad English translation of a bad Spanish translation of neo-Marxist German, but means simply that one is morally obligated to look at things from the viewpoint of the poor. Fair enough. After all, it was Dr. Johnson, not exactly a premature Marxist, who said that "a decent provision for the poor is the true test of civilization."

In focusing on this particular criterion for defining successful development I am invoking, of course, the ideal of equity; but I am *not* invoking "equality," a utopian category that can only obfuscate the moral issues. It is inequitable and immoral that, next door to each other, some human beings are starving while others gorge themselves. To make this situation more equitable and thus morally tolerable, the starvation must stop and the poor must become richer. This goal can be attained without the rich becoming poorer. In other words, I do not assume the need for a leveling of income distribution. Western societies (including the United States) have demonstrated that dramatic improvements are possible in the condition of the poor

24

without great changes in income distribution; the poor can get richer even while the rich get richer too. And there are good economic grounds for thinking that income-leveling policies in the Third World inhibit growth, with the poor paying the biggest price for this inhibition. "Equality" is an abstract and empirically murky ideal; it should be avoided in assessing the success or failure of development strategies.

Third criterion: development cannot be called successful if the achievements of economic growth and equitable distribution come at the price of massive violations of human rights. This criterion applies to both of the calculi formulated in *Pyramids of Sacrifice*. In 1974 it seemed to me and to many others that China offered an illustration of the "calculus of pain." We now know that the economic and egalitarian achievements of Maoism were themselves largely fictitious. Still, I believe that I was correct to insist that, *even if* it were true that Maoism had vanquished hunger among China's poor, this achievement could not morally justify the horrors inflicted by the regime—horrors that entailed the killing of millions of human beings and the imposition of a merciless totalitarian rule on the survivors.

As for the "calculus of meaning," Iran now offers a good instance. The Shah's regime undoubtedly achieved economic growth, it ameliorated the condition of many of the poor (even if a corrupt elite greatly enriched itself in the process), and its violations of human rights, ugly though they were, did not come even close to the horrors of Maoism (not to mention the nightmare of terror of the Khomeini regime). However, as Grace Goodell has persuasively argued, the reform program of the Shah systematically trampled on the mores and values by which the largest number of Iranians gave meaning to their lives. It was a program of rapid and coercive modernization, contemptuous of tradition and of indigenous institutions. Logically enough, this alliance of technocrats, profiteers, and secret police evoked a neotraditionalist reaction. The tragic consequences following the triumph of these reactionaries, and the fact that the new regime has worsened the condition of the Iranian people, cannot provide an *ex post facto* justification of the Shah's policies. (By analogy, the Bolshevik Revolution was a catastrophe for the Russian people; but it does not follow from this that czarism, though in many ways morally superior to its successor regime, was a wise and humane system.)

It should be clear what I mean by "massive violations of human rights": mass killings, concentration camps, forced deportations, torture, separation of families, pervasive intimidation—in other words, the standard practices of 20th-century totalitarianism. But I should

25

stress at the same time that I do *not* include democracy as a necessary element in this criterion for successful development. Democracy is the best available form of government in the modern world; moreover, I consider it the only reliable protection of human rights under modern conditions.* In the long run, I also believe that democracy and development are necessarily linked realities. All the same, the case regrettably cannot be made that democracy is indispensable to successful development.

Armed with these criteria for development we may now turn to the evidence that has accumulated over the last ten years. Perhaps the most important piece of evidence is negative: the absence of even a single successful case of socialist development in the Third World.

Even in the early 1970s it should not have been news that socialism is not good for economic growth, and also that it shows a disturbing propensity toward totalitarianism (with its customary accompaniment of terror). What has become clearer is that socialism even fails to deliver on its own egalitarian promises (the second criterion of success). In country after country, socialist equality has meant a leveling down of most of the population, which is then lorded over by a highly privileged and by no means leveled elite.

Put simply, socialist equality is shared poverty by serfs, coupled with the monopolization of both privilege and power by a small (increasingly hereditary) aristocracy. That this was so of the Soviet Union had already been accepted by most Western and Third World leftists by the late 1960s and early 1970s. What is evident now is that a Soviet-style *nomenklatura* seems to spring up predictably wherever socialism extends. It has done so in China, in Vietnam, in Cuba, and in such lesser socialist experiments as Angola and Mozambique. None of these countries, not even Cuba, is directly or entirely under Soviet rule. It seems to be the intrinsic genius of socialism to produce these modern facsimiles of feudalism.

The fact that there is not a single case of economically successful and nontotalitarian socialism has begun to sink in. (The social democracies of the West, of course, should not be subsumed under the category of socialism.) The monumental failures of Maoism, failures proclaimed to the world not by its old enemies but directly from Peking, have made a deep impression in Asia; so have the horrors of the triumphant socialist revolution in Indochina. In Asia more than elsewhere in the Third World, there now seems a new openness to

---

*I have explained why at some length in "Democracy for Everyone?," *Commentary*, September 1983.

the possibility of capitalist models, even if the word itself is avoided in favor of circumlocutions like "market mechanisms" or euphemisms like "pluralism." The radical shift from a socialist to a capitalist model in Sri Lanka illustrates this tendency, especially because it came about as the result of open debate and democratic politics.

Two cases touched upon in *Pyramids of Sacrifice*, Peru and Tanzania, are interesting in this connection. The socialist experiments of the Velasco regime ended in economic disaster, after which, prudently, the military handed the mess back to a civilian government that stopped the experiments. It is not clear, however, to what extent the brief and limited socialist policies of the Velasco regime can be blamed for economic problems that antedated it.

The case of Tanzania—an economic fiasco—is much more instructive. Here was a country that in the early 1970s had much going for it—reasonably good resources (especially in agriculture); a dubiously democratic but relatively humane government led by Julius Nyerere, an intelligent and attractive leader by most standards; and freedom from foreign domination. What is more, Tanzania had long been the darling of development-aid institutions, which poured vast amounts of money into the country. Whatever else one may say about the economic and political failures of Tanzania, these cannot be blamed on corrupt leadership, on bad Soviet influence, or on the hostility or destabilizing policies of Western capitalism. The fiasco was self-made.

Tanzania's much-vaunted Ujamaa program of socialist agriculture has come close to destroying the agricultural productivity of the country. As the program has failed economically, it has become more coercive. The government had at first tried to persuade peasants to move to Ujamaa villages by means of incentives; by the late 1970s, pressure had to be applied. As for the non-agricultural sector of the economy, small enough to begin with, the "para-statal organizations" that operate it have succeeded in running that little into the ground. This particular failure has been augmented by systematic pressures on the Indian minority, who (in Tanzania as in other East African countries) comprise much of the small entrepreneurial class. Not surprisingly, the economic failures have gone hand in hand with increasing political repressiveness; Tanzania today is even less democratic and certainly less humane than it was in 1974.

Events in China and Brazil, the two countries discussed at greatest length in *Pyramids of Sacrifice*, have been momentous. In the book I rejected the Maoist model because of its human costs; now the model must also be rejected because of the costs brought about by economic

27

and social mismanagement. To put it differently, where I rejected Maoism on non-Maoist grounds, now the Maoist experiment can be shown to have failed even by its own criteria of success.

Brazil is a more complicated case. Before the oil shock and the ensuing indebtedness crisis, there were some modest signs of a more equitable distribution of the benefits of growth. There has also been an impressive move from harsh military dictatorship toward democracy. It is noteworthy that Fernando Henrique Cardoso, the father of Latin American "dependency theory," is today a federal senator of the largest opposition party and speaks more in the moderate tones of Swedish social democracy than in the fiery neo-Marxist rhetoric of the early 1970s. All the same, by the criteria set forth above, Brazil cannot be cited as a case of successful development, and cannot (yet) be used as an argument for capitalism.

One other case in the Americas, that of Jamaica, is interesting because it (like Sri Lanka) abruptly veered from a socialist to a capitalist course, and did so as a result of democratic politics. Jamaica, however, is beset with manifold troubles; the capitalist experiment of the Seaga regime is still very new; and the place of the experiment remains uncertain.

A number of other cases (such as the Ivory Coast) are sometimes cited in favor of capitalism. But these aside, the most dramatic and convincing success stories today, and the ones offering the strongest brief for capitalism, are in East Asia.

There is, first of all, the astounding instance of Japan. To be sure, Japan is no longer regarded as anything but a highly advanced industrial society—in some ways a more successful one than the societies of North America and Western Europe. This very achievement, however, is what makes Japan crucial for any responsible theory of development. Here is the only non-Western society that has moved from underdevelopment to full-blown modernity within the span of a century. Moreover, whatever variables may have been in play (political, cultural, geographical, and so on), Japan is a successful *capitalist* society. How did the Japanese pull this off? And can others learn from their success? Not surprisingly, Third World politicians and intellectuals, even in countries that have reason to fear Japanese power, such as those of Southeast Asia, talk of the "Japanese model" as something to be admired and emulated.

But Japan no longer stands alone as a success story. There are the four countries of what may be called the Asian prosperity crescent— South Korea, Taiwan, Hong Kong, and Singapore. Despite important differences among them, each has employed an exuberantly capitalist strategy to move out of underdevelopment to the newly designated status of "New Industrialized Country" (or NIC). And this has happened with breathtaking speed and thoroughness, within the span of two decades. In no meaningful sense can these countries any longer be regarded as parts of the Third World (though Hong Kong, depending on China's policy toward it, may fall back into underdevelopment in the near future). There are even grounds for thinking that their prosperity is pushing into other countries, especially in Southeast Asia (Malaysia, Thailand, and possibly Indonesia).

South Korea, Taiwan, Hong Kong, and Singapore are successful by all three of the criteria listed above. Their rates of economic growth continue to be remarkable. They have completely wiped out Third-World-type misery within their borders. What is more, they (especially Taiwan and South Korea) have forcefully challenged the so-called "Kuznets curve" by combining high growth with a highly egalitarian income distribution. Their regimes, while not democratic, are authoritarian in a generally benign way (especially when compared with others in the region).

These four countries, only one of which, the Republic of Singapore, operates within the United Nations system, are increasingly attracting the attention of analysts of development and are more and more frequently cited as examples to be emulated. They constitute the most important evidence in favor of a capitalist path of development.

What, then, do we know today about development? We know, or should know, that socialism is a mirage that leads nowhere, except to economic stagnation, collective poverty, and various degrees of tyranny. We also know that capitalism has been dramatically successful, if in a limited number of underdeveloped countries. Needless to say, we also know that capitalism has failed in a much larger number of cases. What we do *not* know is why this is so.

It seems to me that the issue of socialism should be put aside for good in any serious discussion of development; it belongs, if anywhere, to the field of political pathology or *Ideologiekritik*. The question that should be of burning urgency (theoretical as well as practical) is why capitalism has succeeded in some places and failed in others. What are the variables of success and failure? That is the crucial question.

The success stories of East Asia have, very understandably, led some analysts to think that an important causal factor may be the culture of the region. A "post-Confucianist hypothesis" proposes that all the successful societies and ethnic groups (notably the overseas Chinese) share a common economic ethic derived from Confucianism, deemed to be a functional equivalent of Max Weber's famous

29

"Protestant ethic." But Confucianism is by no means the only cultural element that may be relevant. Others may include the political traditions of East Asia, patterns of family and household, and different components of the area's religious heritage (such as Mahayana Buddhism).

One does not have to de a disciple of Weber to want these hypotheses addressed. Indeed, if one is concerned with Third World development in general, one would dearly love to see them falsified—not out of antagonism toward East Asia, but because the East Asian success stories can only become models for other parts of the world if they do not hinge on a non-exportable cultural factor. One might advise an African country to adopt the economic policies of South Korea; one can hardly advise the Africans to adopt Korean culture.

In *Pyramids of Sacrifice* I put forward a "postulate of ignorance": we are compelled to act politically even when we do not know many of the factors determining the situation in which we find ourselves. I formulated this postulate in the context of recommending a non-doctrinaire approach to development policy. I would reiterate it today. We are less ignorant than we were ten years ago, but there is still much that we do not know. Those charged with political responsibility in the matter of development, however, do not have the luxury of the social scientist who can always say that more research is needed. Science is, in principle, infinitely patient; politicians must act out of the urgencies of the moment. In such a situation the morally sensitive politician should be fully conscious of the fact that, whatever he chooses to do—and often the range of choices is narrow—he will be gambling. The evidence today strongly suggests that it is much safer to bet on capitalism.

Democracy and Human Rights

Michael Novak

Introduction

Nowadays, when a nation calls itself a Popular Democratic Republic, we often understand that it is neither a Republic nor a democracy. We suspect that is not even popular. So we know, today more than ever, that words do not a democracy make. Of what, then, is a democracy composed? More important, in its absence, how does one *create* a democracy?

Of the world's 160 current regimes, only about twenty—surely, not more than thirty—are true democracies, whose respect for human rights we honor. Chile, alas, is not now one of them, although its government publicly and privately declares that Chile is in a "period of transition towards democracy." What practical steps should a Catholic theologian visiting Chile recommend during such a period? This is a question I must face—before God and before you.

One of the great strengths of democratic thinking is that it is *practical*. Democracy is a *praxis*, not a theory. As a practice, it has two locations: one in the *habits* and dispositions of a people, and one in a set of living *institutions* and functioning procedures. James Madison pointed to the first when he said that the American Constitution has existence, not on paper, but in the habits and dispositions of the American people. A Constitution is not, first of all, a written document but a people's way of life. Tonight I mean to stress that theme. Any people who wish to create a stable democracy must learn to practice certain specific democratic *virtues*.

The second theme I wish to stress is that democracy lives not only in specific habits but in specific *institutions*. Habits are not enough: institutions are required. Even a virtuous people will suffer under poor political institutions. Many analysts of democracy today fail to stress the central importance of building specific institutions. So tonight I want to stress a second thesis: that human rights can only be defended by certain working institutions. I have, then, two theses;

we need to concentrate on building democratic *habits* and democratic *institutions.*

At the same time, I wish to stress a third thesis: the social teaching of the Roman Catholic church, which has long and valuable traditions, needs to become more specific about strengthening the habits and institutions of *democracy* and of economic *development.* In short, Catholic social teaching needs fresh development, just as in fact it undergoes constant development. Recently I read, for example, a statement by Padre Renato Hevia, S.J., in *El Mercurio* (3/13/83), in which this good Jesuit took sharp issue with the traditional way of imagining the pastoral role of a priest. "No," he said, "the pastoral is not only the spiritual, . . . The pastoral is everything that contributes to the humanization of men. Everything which contributes to the enlargement and the realization of his humanity, of his dignity, goes in the line of the Gospel." We see, then, there is a traditional way of understanding Catholic social teaching and a way which is newly being developed. My own thesis is that the new developments, suggested by Father Hevia, do not go far enough.

From my point of view, the traditional Catholic teaching was adapted to the *ancien regime.* That regime was led, both in Europe and in Latin America, by three social classes chiefly: the landed aristocracy, the generals, and the clergy. Under that regime, it was imagined that the wealth of the world was finite; there was no question of development. And, clearly, the social order was not democratic.

In a parallel way, the new social teaching also has little to say about the practical virtues and institutions necessary for democratic living and essential to producing economic development. The new social theology of "humanization" is too general; it is a new antithesis to a thesis. It is not yet a synthesis.

The traditional theology was private; liberation theology is social. The traditional theology seemed to concentrate upon the next world; the new social theology seems to concentrate upon this world. The traditional theology was addressed in clear words to the aristocracy and to the military, concerning charity; the new social theology is still being addressed to the aristocracy and military, but now concerning social justice. The traditional theology did not promise the production of new wealth, however, and neither does the new social theology. Both ignore the middle class, the persons of commerce and industry who produce new wealth and are the chief creators of democracy, and who include labor among them.

I cannot analyze the two earlier forms of theology further. Subtleties and distinctions would need to be added. Yet my thesis stands.

Neither the traditional theology nor the new social theology meets our immediate and long-term needs. If we wish to produce both democracy and economic development: (1) which *virtues* do we need to practice and (2) which *institutions* do we need to establish? These are questions of *praxis*. Christian faith is fertile with materials for these necessities.

My first lecture, therefore, will be on the institutions and virtues of political democracy. My second will be on the institutions and virtues of economic development. Democracy and development— these are new possibilities for Catholic social teaching. They have not yet been adequately faced. Yet Pope John Paul II, in speaking of "Creation Theology" (in *Laborem Exercens*), shows us how to approach creation creatively—as co-creators with God.

Permit me also to say a word about my intellectual roots. I intend to revivify and to expand the intellectual work of Jacques Maritain, particularly such books of his as *Christianity and Democracy, Man and the State, Integral Humanism,* and *Reflections on America.* You may assume that his philosophy and his theology are mine. Nonetheless, there are two omissions in Maritain's work which I would like to fill: (1) Maritain says far too little about economics, and, therefore, about the problem of economic development. That is why I have focused these lectures on "Democracy and Development." (2) Maritain says too little about *how* to create democracy where it is absent: he seems to have had more in mind the condition of political crisis in Western Europe and less that of Asia, Africa, and Latin America.

The second mentor I should mention is James Madison, who, along with Alexander Hamilton and John Jay, presents in *The Federalist* the most sustained body of practical reflection on how to construct a democracy that the world has yet seen. Like Aristotle's *Nicomachean Ethics, The Federalist* represents a move from *theoria* to *phronesis*, from science to practical wisdom. James Madison is one of the great thinkers of the Americas. His work is indispensable for builders of democracy. Latin Americans too much neglect him.

The third source on which I would draw, a challenge for those of us who share a Catholic tradition, is the great Protestant theologian, Reinhold Niebuhr, especially in his books *The Nature and Destiny of Man, Moral Man and Immoral Society, The Irony of American History,* and *Man's Nature and His Communities.* There is a tendency in Catholic thought, with its emphasis on natural law, the Absolute, and the organic corporative society, to overlook the ambiguities, ironies, self-deceptions, paradoxes, competitions, pluralistic currents and unintended consequences of human intentions and actions. Here, without deviating at all from Catholic-Christian orthodoxy, Catholic thinkers may find important correctives. The work of Niebuhr teaches us to see ambiguity in our own purposes, to see kernels of truth in the positions we oppose, and to advance mutual purposes by just compromise and adjustment. For this world is not the world of perfect, but only of approximate, justice. In such a world, compromise *with persons* is not the same as a compromise *of principle*; it is a just recognition of our limited natures, and a mark of respect for the humanity in our foes.

Human Rights and Institutions

The human rights celebrated in the International Covenant of Human Rights—in whose articulation Jacques Maritain played an important role—have only one realistic defense: the actual functioning of democratic institutions. Today, we can assert this as an empirical proposition rather than as a theoretical one. In 1949, there were only forty-nine nations on this small planet. Today there are 160: 160 diverse experiments in political economy. In only about twenty to thirty of these nations can we admire the actual observance of the human rights of citizens. Most nations of the world are still in the grip of tyrannies of one sort or another. In most, human rights are poorly, if at all, defended. In each of those twenty to thirty nations ranked high for their observance of human rights, democratic institutions guarantee that observance. I stress the central importance of institutions.

As James Madison pointed out, the human rights of citizens are not defended by the words of a constitution, not by "parchment barriers," but by two barriers of a quite different sort: (1) by *institutions* of due process and (2) by *free associations* of individuals able to insist that those institutions do function as they are intended to function. Poland subscribes to the International Covenant; its own Constitution is eloquent about human rights. On paper, the rights of Polish citizens and workers are defended. But beyond paper? Do institutions function as paper says they should? Are free associations able to *insist* that those institutions function? Between words and realities two barriers are missing: institutions and free associations.

In the United States, blacks had rights on paper, and institutions of human rights did function; but only when, in the Civil Rights movement, free associations of individuals insisted that those institutions function for blacks as for others did full civil rights actually begin to be observed. *Institutions* and *free associations:* these alone make human rights real in history. These are the reality principles. These are also the real substance of democracy.

34

Let me now enumerate, without being exhaustive, the institutions which give working democracies their reality. Whoever would build democracy must build such institutions.

1. *Free associations.* Without the rights to assemble, to speak and write and to seek together redress of grievances, the governed cannot truly be said to be governed by consent. To be sure, these rights of association do not justify mob rule, and must not be practiced in such a way as to infringe upon the rights of others. These rights depend upon self-respect and also upon respect for others. They depend upon self-restraint and appeal to law. They arise within a system committed to the limited state, ruled by *law* and not by "men"—that is, not by caprice or arbitrary will. Their firm foundation lies in the conviction that rights inhere in individuals and in their free associations, not in states. The rights of states are derivative. God made individuals, made them by nature associative and endowed them and their associations with inalienable rights. States are created by free human beings, *by* their own consent and *within* the limits set by their own autonomous dignity. Without freedom of association, there is no effective consent of the governed.

2. *Independent courts of justice* are indispensable. One cannot trust executive or administrative officials always to do justice; every human being sometimes errs. Such errors need redress. Courts bound by the law of the land—and laws bound by the dignity of human persons—are a condition of justice.

3. *Private property.* The liberty of the human person requires material instruments for the very expression of liberty of conscience. This is a law of incarnation. It is the argument by which St. Thomas Aquinas, like Pope John Paul II in *Laborem Exercens,* establishes the right to *private property.* The right to private property flows from the right to liberty of conscience; conscience can only express itself through material means. The right to private property should, therefore, be understood as a right of the *human spirit,* not as a materialistic proposition. Moreover, its primary force is not so much to empower the person—God has done that—as to *limit the powers of the state.* In this sense, private property is a matter of social justice, not of individual justice; it limits the state. The state cannot invade the liberties of the human person. It cannot, without just cause and legal warrant, enter a person's home. It cannot invade his or her bodily integrity. These points need further comment.

4. A human person is of such *dignity* that the law properly *forbids the state from invading it.* The law places, as it were, a moat around a person's home and property, defending it against trespass and aggression from the state or any other. The law also places, as it were,

an invisible armor around a person's body. No person may be kidnapped or seized against his or her will. No person's body may be touched or injured or, God forbid, tortured. These are crimes against the person.

Abuses of human rights are sometimes defended in the name of survival. But those who uphold Western values cannot use this defense. Every nation sometimes sins. Yet a pattern of human rights abuses is immoral in itself, injures Western values, injures any cause a regime holds dear, and injures that regime's national security. For in any future military emergency, public opinion in democratic nations will not permit their governments to assist such regimes. Thus, abuses of human rights injure the regime which permits them, even more deeply than they injure their victims. In this sense, respect for human rights is a shield which protects regimes, even as it protects their citizens.

5. Another critical institution is a system for the *election* of executive and legislative officers. Elections are no magic wand. But they are clearly far more than symbols, symbolic actions, or merely formal procedures. For they do achieve three real effects. First, elections often result in *removing from office* those of whom the citizens do not approve. This is all too real, as leaders who do not face elections starkly recognize. Second, elections *exhibit* the consent of the governed, *convey legitimacy* to officials, and bring officials into an *office of service* to the people. This liturgical reenactment of fundamental convictions about the true source of political power—in the consent of the governed—is as important to democratic living as the Eucharist to Catholic living. Third, elections provide for a clear, *orderly and regular succession* of power. This is a major factor in the stability of societies. Nations which have not solved the problem of succession reveal not only radical instability but also confusion about the source of legitimate political power. In sum, elections are not magic; but they do have real consequences. They provide ways to express opposition, through ballots rather than through bullets; peaceful ways to bring reform and changes, rather than through terror. They exhibit the dignity of human beings as rational, choosing persons, and the dignity of politics as a vocation of civil argument, loyal opposition, and reasoned diversity of views.

6. *Free labor unions.* One of the most potent of all institutions in any democracy is a free labor union, as a school of democracy and forensic talent for many. The contrasting experience of Great Britain and other western Democracies suggests that labor unions achieve better results when they do not themselves form a political party, but

are active within all parties. The realism and practicality of labor union associations are invaluable in forming a national pool of insight, intelligence, and consensus. Regimes blind to labor blind themselves. The free speech and free press of free labor unions are, typically, an immense source of national patriotism.

7. *Political Parties.* Without political parties, human polities can scarcely learn what their disagreements are, let alone how they might be solved, through consensus. Democracy without political parties would be like lips without sound, or pens without ink; articulation would be impossible. Humans are incarnate persons. Causes need to be personified. Large, vague movements need to be refined into political programs. No "transition to democracy" can be realistic which does not permit parties to begin to function, to exercise, and to learn the arts of responsible action.

8. *A loyal opposition.* I sometimes have the impression that Latin countries, in particular, have trouble with the institution of loyal opposition. Is the Catholic tradition of absolutism too strong? Is "love thine enemy" too difficult a task? Is the spirit of empirical inquiry, pragmatic adjustment, and compromise with persons overpowered by a desire for ideological purity and moral passion? In any case, the distinction between moral passion and political passion is an important one. In politics, one must always assume that one's opponent is also moral, and that in his error there is some truth, as in one's own truth there is always some error. Respect for the loyal opposition is actually for oneself. No institution is more necessary to democratic living. None requires so high a sense of self-criticism, genuine humility, and respect for others. Without benevolence, fellow-feeling, sympathy, a sense of fair play, and other moral sentiments, democracy can be no brotherhood: only fratricide.

9. In general, the democratic way of living teaches *that government by law* rather than by arbitrary will is possible to humankind. Its institutions afford respect for laws greater than any single human will, whether individual or collective. The principles of law which it respects are substantive, not formal, for they honor the capacities for reasoned choice in every single voter. They honor a government of consent, not of coercion: they honor the liberty of free persons to disagree and yet to cooperate. They honor argument for principles, combined with compromise in practical actions with others who fight for different principles. These are not "formalities" only. They are based upon substantive respect for persons of good will who profoundly disagree in judgment. No two human beings are alike. A society of humans is neither a hive nor a herd. Persons disagree. Free

societies bring harmony from difference—not, of course, without immense effort at conciliation.

Utopian Revolution versus Realistic Revolution

Most societies on this planet today are not democracies. Yet in thinking about how to create democracies tomorrow where today they do not exist, utopian revolutionaries differ dramatically from realistic revolutionaries. Invariably, utopian revolutionaries hold that evil situations are evil because of some flaw in *structure*—because of some malevolent other party, class, tyrant, or social arrangement, which, once removed, will allow justice to ensue. The evil, they think, lies not in the hearts of humans but in some identifiable obstacle. Consequently, utopian revolutionaries glorify the moment of revolution, the destruction of their chosen foe, the exaltation of victory. Their favorite self-image is of the rebel brandishing a submachine gun on the barricades and joyously shouting: *"Avanti!"*

The realistic revolutionary has an altogether different diagnosis and an altogether different focus. The realistic revolutionary observes that nearly all social systems fail—fail in producing bread, fail in producing liberty. Thus, the realist diagnoses the multiple causes of such failure. Far from glorifying the revolutionary moment, the realistic revolutionary focuses upon *what will happen after the revolution.* The utopian fantasy is the destruction of (easily identified) evil. A realistic revolution requires the creation of democratic *institutions* worthy of human complexity, respectful of human ambiguity and differences of opinion, and prescient about the many sources of human corruption. The fundamental source of every evil, realists hold, lies in the human heart, even of the revolutionary. Most revolutions in the last two hundred years have resulted in more wretchedness and worse tyranny than originally gave them birth, as Hannah Arendt notes in *On Revolution.*

In this respect, the realistic revolutionary has a decisive advantage. He or she holds fast to the Principle of Peccability. This principle—which might theologically be called the doctrine of sin or, empirically, a survey of all the ways in which historical regimes fall short of the dignity of humankind—has two parts: (1) Every person sometimes sins: therefore, trust no person with too much power; divide all powers. (2) Most persons most of the time are decent, generous, responsible, and good. The first part makes democracy (and capitalism and pluralism) necessary. The second part makes democracy (and capitalism and pluralism) possible.

Let me explain. On the coins of the United States is embossed the motto, "In God we trust." The operational meaning of this expression is "No one else." One must not trust presidents. One must not trust legislators. One must not trust judges. Therefore, the separation of powers; executive, legislative, judicial. But there is a still deeper separation, the separation of *systems.*

A true democracy cannot be imagined in the image of monotheism: one integral, self-contained system. It is properly imagined in the image of the Trinity: three systems united and yet distinct, each *interdependent with* and yet significantly *independent from,* the other two. This separation of systems rests upon two realistic judgments about the history of political economies in this world of sin.

The first is as follows: *Trust no political person or collective to make fundamental decisions about conscience, information, ideas or the life of the spirit.* This judgment leads to the separation of the political system (the state) from the sphere of conscience (the Church and the individual), from the sphere of information (the press) and from the sphere of ideas and the life of the spirit (the university, the philosophers, poets, associations, and persons). In short, there must be at least *two* systems, each with its own institutions, methods, personality types, privileges, rights, and duties: political institutions, on the one hand, and the moral-cultural institutions, on the other.

The second is like the first: *Trust no political person or collective to make all fundamental decisions about economic matters.* This judgment leads to the (relative) separation of the political system from the economic system. In a word, there must be not only two separate systems, but three: a political system, a moral-cultural system, and an economic system. Each, of course, depends upon the other two. Each affects, checks, regulates, even interpenetrates the other two. But each also has substantial independence. Each, indeed, promotes and favors rather different virtues, skills, methods, and habits of judgment. The one body, to borrow the metaphor of St. Paul, has many members. Yet even that image fails, for it is essential that the three separated systems of a thriving democracy be vigilant concerning the other two, check the other two. For this separation rests upon the judgment that every person or collective sometimes sins; no one may be trusted with too much power, especially beyond the limits of his own domain.

I must hasten to add that every single human being lives simultaneously within each of these three systems. Each of us is a political animal, an economic animal, and a seeker after the good and the true. As each person is not divided into three, so the system of three systems is not divided into three. And yet for the protection of the integrity of each person, it is in the world of practice indispensable that the three central powers of human life be placed in the hands of separate institutions and persons.

The conception of three systems in one flows from the Principle of Peccability. In God we trust. No one else.

Confusions about Democracy

As Winston Churchill said, democracy is a flawed and imperfect form of governance, except when compared with the alternatives. Three confusions about democracy also injure it.

First, democracy is not solely a political system; it has immense influence, good and bad, on economic conditions. There is an inevitable temptation, especially in welfare democracies, for politicians to vote for state expenditures on behalf of their constituencies for which the politicians will not have to bear the responsibility to pay. The result is a policy of "tax, tax; spend, spend," leaving the debts to one's successors in office and to future generations. Yet the state cannot spend what it does not have. All modern systems are not merely *political* systems, but systems of political *economy.* Political theory has not quite caught up with the importance of *economic responsibility* in political actors. This is a weakness in classical thought. Far greater *economic* sophistication is required of political theory, especially for democracies, than we have yet acquired.*

Second, classical writers long ago worried that democratic regimes would unleash mob psychology, degenerate into anarchy, and end again in tyranny, usually military tyranny. How often this has happened in history! To prevent this, entire populations need to internalize certain constraints upon passion and behavior. A joke making the rounds of Warsaw in 1981 may exemplify the point. "There are only two solutions to the Polish crisis," it goes, "the miraculous solution and the realistic solution. The realistic solution would be if Our Lady of Czestochowa would suddenly appear, with all the angels and saints, and solve the Polish crisis. The miraculous solution would be if the Poles could learn to cooperate." The discipline exercised by Solidarity in Poland—that marvelous, if now aborted, revolution of reason and bloodlessness—is extraordinary. All peoples who would create democracy need such disciplines. These entail a crucial insight, about which Maritain has written brilliantly. Intuitively, most people think that a nation can only be unified by a single vision, a single set

---

*The field of political economy was only invented in 1776. Yet it took until 1891 before Leo XIII brought the Catholic church to face the social question, and until 1971 before Paul VI recognized the centrality of economic *development* to social justice.

of principles, one theory held in common by all. It is counterintuitive, but true, that a nation can exhibit cooperation and unity *in practice*, even while remaining quite pluralistic in vision, principles, and theory.

To agree to disagree; to cooperate with persons whose views we do not share; to compromise for the sake of cooperation, even while not surrendering one's goal-oriented principles—these are high and historically rare social disciplines. It seems so natural to hold that "If you are not with me one hundred percent, you are against me," that many peoples find cooperative action in practice almost unthinkable. The spirit of practical compromise seems to them like the abandonment of principles, rather than like the judgment, which it is, that in this world societies must move forward step by practical step toward proximate justice, while any effort to attain absolute justice is inevitably murderous. Catholic social teaching must learn to stress this crucial virtue of practical democracy.

Theologically, this world is a world of sin, imperfection, irony, unintended consequences, and tragedy. Therefore, in politics, as Aristotle long ago said, one must be satisfied with a tincture of virtue. To ask too much of politics is to destroy politics. To learn to judge what is prudent and may be accomplished peacefully, and to cooperate with one's ideological foes in accomplishing even that much, is the highest art of politics. It is necessary to hold that, in politics, perfection consists in achieving the imperfect; it is not only imperfect, but murderous, to attempt to achieve the perfect. For ardent souls, these are hard lessons. Democracy, however, is like the plain and humble teaching of the gospels, not like the Second Coming of the Messiah.

A third confusion about democracy is the threat afforded by a tyrannical majority, especially a moralistic majority. Democracy is not simply majority rule. A majority can be a tyrant, too. Any democracy is threatened if it is not sufficiently diverse. James Madison feared, for example, that if the infant United States remained predominantly a nation of farmers, it would be natural to such a majority to believe that its own sense of reality was identical to reality, and to reject dissident views. This would be a danger, above all, in moral matters. Madison's principal remedy is simple and profound: a vital democracy depends upon the promotion of commerce and industry. There are two reasons why this is so. First, uniquely, commerce and industry generate conflicting interests. Typically, what is good for one is onerous for others. Regions have diverse geographical and natural advantages and disadvantages. One industry is a rival to another; so is firm to firm. One technology is rival to another. Wholesalers and retailers have different interests, as have ranchers and farmers, capital-intensive and labor-intensive enterprises, those requiring transport and those close to their markets. Moreover, diverse material interests nurture different personality types and worldviews; dentists are not, typically, like truck drivers, nor are steel manufacturers like librarians. The more diverse the panoply of commercial and industrial interests, the less likely it is that democracy can be captured by a monopolistic majority. Monopoly of any sort is a threat to democracy.

For this reason, incidentally, the American West was opened up by the Homestead Act: encouraging multiple owners of property, rather than recreating the great landed estates of the Holy Roman Empire, on which peasants toiled for a landed aristocracy. The multiplication of material interests is a key to the success of democracy. This is the reason, I believe, why every admirable and functioning democracy in the world today—from Sweden to Great Britain, from Costa Rica to Japan—has a capitalist economic system: private property, reasonably free markets, incentives, a state limited in the economic arena (as in other arenas).

Do not misunderstand me. I hold that a capitalist economy—defined as above—is a necessary but not a sufficient condition for the protection of democracy. One must do more than respect private property and markets; these are, after all, pre-capitalist institutions. One must, as well, limit the powers of the state. And it is crucial to limit, to check, and to prevent dominant monopolies. Authoritarian governments typically fail in these respects—and their economies suffer for those failures. For the key to the sort of capitalism that protects democracy lies in *multiplying* the sources of economic decision making. That is why the democratic state promotes commerce and industry. For the health of democracy, it is fully as necessary to promote economic activism on the part of every able citizen as to promote political activism and cultural activism.

The aim of democracy is to empower every single person through active participation in all three spheres: political, economic, and moral. The root of *capitalism* (the term popularized by Marx) is *caput,* head; and no system is worthy of the name unless it progressively activates head after head, until the number of economic decision makers virtually coincides with the number of citizens. The multiplication of intellect is the key. Diversity of interest, stimulated imagination, and new invention are the means. Only through an active, developing economy can democracy be protected and made to work in the real world of human struggle.

Lessons for Catholic Social Thought

I said at the beginning that I had three theses: first about the virtues and, second, about the institutions required both for democracy and for economic development; and, third, about the new role Catholic social teaching must undertake. By now, I hope my thought is clear. Social teaching adequate to the traditional, static, anti-democratic *ancien regime* is not likely to produce the habits or the institutions of democracy. In my view, socialism in its various forms is a type of nostalgia, looking back toward a medieval sense of community and the organic, corporative society of an earlier period of history. Governments of the left typically have the same authoritarian shape as traditional tyrannies, only with a different ideology and a terrible new efficiency. They produce neither bread nor liberty. For this reason, I have looked for a third way beyond traditional societies and beyond socialism.

Whether or not my own particular recommendation is the correct one, Catholic social teaching must of necessity prepare the Catholic people for democracy. This means instruction in the specifically democratic *virtues*—realism rather than utopianism, respect for individuals and checks upon tyrannical majorities, the Principle of Peccability, the spirit of compromise and of loyal opposition. Political passions must not be allowed to become too hot, for democracy like metal melts when temperatures are too high. Moreover, many sectors of life ought to be kept free from politics and ideology. Political visions should not be metaphysical or religious but limited and realistic, for when politics embraces everything it corrupts such independent goods as truth, the university, journalism, the clergy, the family, and even friendship. The totalization of politics is not virtue, but a primary disease, the incubator of totalitarian practices. Politics, like the state, must be limited.

The *habits* necessary for a working democracy, therefore, must be analyzed, taught, learned and practiced. The role of moral and cultural institutions in building democracies is crucial, fundamental, indispensable. Democracy can take root only in cultures of certain kinds, although all cultures can learn the requisite virtues. For these virtues are natural to the entire human race and may be acquired by all.

Similarly, the *institutions* required as the infrastructure of democracy must also be analyzed, taught, and developed. I want particularly to stress the importance of *economic* institutions in the political economy of democracy. Political freedom without economic freedom is shallow; economic freedom without political freedom is fickle. The two need each other and reinforce each other. Both need the guidance, self-restraint, and institutional checks set upon them by institutions of morals and culture: by a free press, by free universities, by free churches, and by free associations of many sorts.

All three systems work together as one whole: the political system (democratic), the economic system (social market, free, capitalist), and the moral and cultural system (pluralist). For a stable and economically dynamic democracy, all three systems are required, each with its own proper health and in equilibrium with the other two. I call such a threefold system democratic capitalism, but the name is less important than the reality. The social teaching of the Catholic church must, in any case, teach the virtues and help create the *institutions* of democracy and economic dynamism. These are new but vitally important tasks.

Conclusion

In the next lecture, we must turn more directly to the theme of development. Suffice it here to say that we have tried to reflect together on democracy and institutions, especially the institutions of human rights; on realistic as opposed to utopian ways to build democracy; upon the Principle of Peccability and the separation of systems and powers to which it gives rise; on three classic confusions about democracy; and on the urgent tasks of Catholic social teaching in the immediate future.

Democracy works. It has shown itself to be marvelously productive both of bread and of liberty, of cooperation and a spirit of compromise, of humble and yet dramatic human progress—and it is the most powerful aspiration, still, of peoples everywhere. It is a poor form of governance, as befits this poor human race; yet, in comparison with the alternatives, its realism braces the heart. And its roots are ever nourished by the biblical conceptions of the individual conscience, the human community, and the special vocation of Christians not merely to reflect the world, but to change it, building up in it an approximation to the Kingdom of truth and liberty, justice, and love, to which we are called.

This is the first of two lectures Michael Novak gave at the Pontifical University, Santiago, Chile, May 3–5, 1983. Reprinted from *Catholicism in Crisis,* September 1983.

Democracy and Development

Michael Novak

Fix in your mind the year 1800. Then imagine the course of development until today, in the brief period of 183 years.

In 1891, in his encyclical *Rerum Novarum*, Leo XIII turned the attention of the Catholic church to a new problem in Christian history: to the revolution in economics. Consider the poverty of Chile, or that of the United States, in 1891. And yet compared to the picture in 1800, consider how Europe—and the world—had already been transformed.

In 1776, in Britain, the largest factory had twenty employees. In 1820, there were only 220 factories in all of France, most of them small textile plants. Then, with gathering speed, industrialization occurred—for things as small as pins and silk stockings, as homey as Singer sewing machines, as large as locomotives. Human life began to be transformed.

In 1800, there were only 800 million persons on this planet. Today, only 183 years later, this number has grown to 4.4 billion. Moreover, one easily forgets how many poor and hungry ones there were in 1800. Someone has recently said that there are today 750 million hungry persons on this planet. What he did not say is that there were almost certainly that very number of poor and hungry in the year 1800. The difference today is that there are 3.5 billion who are living above the level of subsistence and who are *not* poor and hungry. The task is far from accomplished; but significant progress has been made.

If we use the year 1800 as a benchmark, then we can see that the reality pointed to by the word "development" has by now a history of not quite two hundred years and has not yet run its assigned course. Since 1949 alone, 110 new nations have come into existence. During virtually every decade since the year 1800, one nation and then another has come awake to the possibilities of development. Decade by decade, the various nations continue today to pass various milestones at various statistical levels: infant mortality, individual longevity, literacy, annual per capita income, years of education, the acquisition of technical and political skills, religious liberty, the building of institutions of human rights, and other measurements of human development. Not all nations move with equal speed past these milestones. Some dart ahead very quickly, and others, once moving briskly, suddenly begin for a while to decline. Some seem to move with immense lethargy, inefficiency, corruption even, and a certain hopelessness; others, equally poor at the beginning and often even more unfavored by nature, make steady and dramatic gains. The nations are not equal. The course of development is not uniform. For every nation, even the most advanced, there is yet a long way to traverse, as measured against our own ideals.

But whence come our ideals? The very idea of "development" is something that took a long time to "develop" in history. In many respects, Adam Smith was the very first to imagine a political economy based upon the imperative of development. He saw the immense poverty and misery of the world, and believed that it was not necessary. He was the first to foresee a world made interdependent and united in productive pursuits, lawlike, pacific, and dynamic. With this vision began a great revolution. Karl Marx described it as follows:

> The bourgeoisie, during its rule of scarce one hundred years, has created more massive and more colossal productive forces than have all preceding generations together. Subjection of Nature's forces to man, machinery, application of chemistry to industry and agriculture, steam navigation, railways, electric telegraphs, clearing of whole continents for cultivation, canalization of rivers, whole populations conjured out of the ground—what earlier century had even a presentiment that such productive forces slumbered in the lap of social labor?

Recently, the American democratic socialist writer Michael Harrington has expressed concern about the possibilities of socialism in the Third World, on the grounds that one cannot simply "socialize poverty." By contrast, the vision with which Adam Smith began was indeed a vision of almost universal poverty. The ideals behind democratic capitalism—that system which would be at once democratic in polity, capitalist in economy, and pluralistic in its moral and cultural institutions—was precisely designed to overcome poverty. Its aim was to unleash the creativity which the Creator had implanted in the human breast, making every human being a co-creator with Him. John Locke had observed that if one took the field in Britain most favored by nature, favored in the quality of its soil, its inclination toward the sun, its positioning for the weather, and the like, and at the end of the year counted up its harvest as yielded by nature itself, and, then, in the next year, applied to that same field the best of agricultural science even in the seventeenth century, one would find that that yield could be increased not simply twice, nor even by ten times, but by one hundred times. In other words, Locke concluded, nature has hidden within it far greater riches, placed there by the Creator, than it has yet entered into the wit of man to derive from it. The task of human beings is to become co-creators with God, and to discover in nature the secrets which nature's Creator has hidden there. This is the vision which, implicitly, Pope John Paul II takes up in the opening pages of *Laborem Exercens.* He speaks about "the theology of creation."

It is important to recognize that recent popes, especially Pope Paul VI, have begun to pick up Adam Smith's theme of development. They have completed the thought of Leo XIII by adding to it a world perspective, and also by adding to it the perspective of development. They, too, almost two centuries after Adam Smith, have begun to imagine one interdependent world, moving toward an ever fuller development of the possibilities hidden within it by the Creator.

Adam Smith called his book (1776) not the "Wealth of Individuals," nor even "The Wealth of Scotland" or Great Britain, but, rather, *An Inquiry Into the Nature and Causes of the Wealth of Nations*—the wealth of *all* nations. His vision is of the human race as one community, a vision which will not be fulfilled until a sound material base has been placed under every single human being on this planet.

This vision has brought about a revolution in our ethics. Most treatises of ethics, under the heading of political economy, ever since the time of Aristotle and continuing on into our own time, treat the subject chiefly under the heading "distributive justice." The assumption behind this heading is that the wealth of the world is both finite and known. The only remaining moral problem is how to distribute it. The insights of Adam Smith, and the real historical processes to which he pointed, changed all this. For now, confronting the actual poverty and misery of most of the world in the year 1776, and recognizing that human beings at last knew how to create new wealth, Adam Smith envisaged a new moral imperative. If there are so many poor and hungry, and if the human race can produce enough new wealth so that this poverty and hunger is no longer necessary, then, surely, we have a new moral obligation to *produce* such new wealth. In other words, there comes into existence something which might be called "productive ethics," or the moral *obligation* of nations to develop.

Development, in a word, has acquired moral force. It is an imperative laid upon the entire human race. And one must now begin to study how this obligation is to be acquitted. It is not enough simply to have good intentions. If there are human beings suffering, and if new wealth may be created to alleviate this suffering, then one must struggle in the real world to bring about actual development. Those who act in the field of political economy must be judged not only by their intentions but also by the results they achieve. Ideas have consequences. Consequences matter.

Let us go back to consider how the world was changing between the generation during which Adam Smith wrote in 1776, and the generation in which John Stuart Mill wrote his *Principles of Political Economy* in 1848. Mill remarks that in his own living memory and that of his contemporaries, there were many landed aristocrats in Britain who were, in essence, consumers of their own wealth. They raised private armies. They erected grand castles and country homes. They managed large estates. They held sumptuous parties, balls, and entertainments. They supported large retinues. Mill observed that in former times even the ordinary people worked less hard than in the era in which he was actually writing. Their labors were many during the planting season and during the harvesting, but during the winter there were many long leisure hours and, indeed, often during the summer it was the same. But by 1848, more and more of the population were beginning to commit themselves to much longer hours of labor, and throughout the year. They deserved, he said, to receive recompense for this labor, whether or not the fruits of it were sold and for whatever price. They deserved a just wage.

On the other hand, more and more of the wealthy were discovering that it is not good enough simply to inherit wealth and to consume it; it is far better to invest it, to turn it to productive use, and to create new wealth. Thus, more and more wealth was being invested in new factories and new commercial enterprises of many sorts. Those who invested these funds, which had an obvious social and productive use, not only for themselves and for their laborers, but for the entire society, had a right, Mill thought, to have their investment repaid over the years. To recompense them for the time during which they did not spend these funds upon themselves, but rather invested them, they also had a right to a reasonable rate of return. Mill justified the *wages of labor* by the sacrifices of their own leisure which working men and women were willing to make. He justified a *return on investment* by the sacrifice of consumption and the risk which investors were willing to make. Indeed, this is how Mill distinguished capital from wealth: capital is productive, wealth alone is not.

Mill's fundamental insight, like Smith's, was that new wealth might be created. Thus, the national capital of Great Britain need not be in 1790 what it had been in 1780, or in 1848 what it had been in 1838. Indeed, for the first time in human history, a single nation was exhibiting a steady increment in national capital in virtually every single year, for a chain of years unbroken for much longer than a century. In other words, the word "progress" was no longer simply a dream, but was an obvious fact being accomplished day by day, tangibly and visibly.

One recalls that one of the villains of earlier literature had been the miser. Why was the miser conceived to be a villain? In the days when it seemed that wealth was limited and known, and when wealth was identified simply as the holding of gold, then anyone who "sat in his counting house counting up his money" was selfishly subtracting from the limited common store. This act of vanity and selfishness did in fact deprive others, when wealth was so limited. But, after Balzac, the figure of the miser as an archetype of evil disappears from literature. For once the insight had become established that new wealth can be created, and that wealth consists not in gold but in the inventive ideas and the products of human intellect which lead to productive investment, then the miser came to be seen not as a villain but as a fool. Instead of investing his wealth and thus creating new wealth, he was simply hoarding it. The miser became a figure of ridicule rather than of villainy.

It is important to see that development, if it means anything at all, means the creation of new wealth. It is a creative act. And it is rooted in intellect. Most of the things we today call resources were not known to be resources two hundred years ago. It was in 1809 that a man outside of Philadelphia figured out how to ignite anthracite coal; that such coal burned hotter and longer than bituminous coal was well known, but the obstacle had been how to achieve a way of igniting it quickly and steadily. Once this secret had been learned, the anthracite coal fields of my native state of Pennsylvania (about which I have written on the struggle of the United Mine Workers in *The Guns of Lattimer*) were opened, steam travel on the oceans became possible, and also the railways and the heating of skyscrapers. It was in 1859 that the first oil well was dug in Titusville, Pennsylvania, and in 1878 that the first electric light was illuminated in New Jersey. So it is also with the use of natural gas and the discovery of electrical power through nuclear energy. And so it is also throughout entire fields of

49

chemistry, electronics, metallurgy, and many others. The human mind is the primary source of wealth. The inquiry which Adam Smith began into the nature *and causes* of the wealth of nations leads in every place to intellect, to inventiveness, to creativity.

But how does one design an entire society so that it will promote invention and creativity? Crucial in this process is the law of patents and the right to royalties. These new *institutions* provided both a structure of law and a system of incentives making it worthwhile for inventors to dedicate many years of research to developing new resources, processes, and products. Further, it is important that new ideas, once invented, do not remain solely in the laboratory, in the university, or in the private knowledge of the inventor. It is important to move them as quickly as possible into production and distribution. For this, too, institutions are necessary.

I observed earlier that the vision of Adam Smith was not the vision of an individualist. It is a vision of the universal human family, in all the nations on this planet. I want to observe now that the production of wealth is also social. It depends on the existence of certain kinds of *institutions,* and on the *cooperation* of a great many diverse persons and institutions. There must first be a structure of law, and this is a social achievement. There must next be institutions like the patent office, and institutions which support discovery and invention. These, too, are social achievements. Finally, modern economic tasks are so complex that they cannot be achieved by one individual alone. Further, these institutions must be such that they will endure longer than the life of any one *generation*, for economic tasks are also too large for any one generation alone. In order to achieve new economic tasks, one must create new social institutions.

Fortunately, there was available a model for the development of such institutions. From the burial societies of ancient Egypt through the monasteries of Western Europe, there had developed a body of law for incorporated associations. As many monks banded together under St. Benedict, and as the monasteries continued from generation to generation, so also there had developed a body of law to regularize the relation of these new institutions to the rest of society. This body of law afforded the legal precedents for the development of corporations committed to economic tasks. These voluntary associations came to be known as business corporations.

When Adam Smith was writing, a large proportion of business corporations in Great Britain and elsewhere were conceived as monopoly grants from the crown, as though all economic rights inhered in the state, and these monopoly grants were given in recognition of services rendered to the crown. One frequently encounters reminders of this circumstance in the inscription on products from Great Britain: "By appointment of her majesty." In the infant United States, by contrast, as the historian Oscar Handlin has pointed out, there were already by the year 1800 more private business corporations than in all of Great Britain, indeed in all of the world combined. All that was required for their formation was that individual men and women make a contract with one another to accomplish certain economic tasks.

The state did not create business corporations. They were voluntary associations. They had standing in law, which was recognized by the state and by all individuals. But what I most wish to stress is that business corporations are *social* institutions. The primary mover in the economic system of democratic capitalism is not the individual, although that is what some ideology would lead one to think, but rather the voluntary *association.* The corporation is a *social* organization. It develops and nurtures its own form of community, different from the spontaneous community of the pre-capitalist village. This new community is partial, voluntary, associative, cooperative, and utterly dependent upon a high degree of social skills among its many members. It has as its preconditions many spiritual qualities. To make it function, its participants must practice many spiritual, moral, and social disciplines. It depends upon a respect for law and a capacity to cooperate well and easily with others. As against familism, it depends upon a certain objectivity and recognition of due process and internal regulation.

Finally, business corporations can only function within political systems of certain sorts. Their existence and their success depends to an extraordinary degree upon the character of the law. To function well, business corporations depend upon many sorts of governmental regulation; all competitors must be held to similar rules. The law must have sufficient stability to allow long-term contracts to be entered into without excessive anxiety.

A capitalist economic system is often presented as a system based upon individualism. One can see how this happened. Invention and creative ideas normally do occur to one person at one time. One can see why emphasis is placed upon individual initiative and individual imagination. But the larger truth is that no idea can be brought into reality except through the complex process of economic activities, and these activities are in the most important respects social and even communitarian. They depend upon a great deal of trust as between individuals, respect for law, mutual cooperation and mutual dedication. The aristocrat tends to be a much more highly developed, not to say eccentric, *individual* than does the person who succeeds at making a business corporation function well. The most original invention of democratic capitalism is not the individual but, rather, the voluntary business corporation. This is a social invention.

This is not the end of the matter. I have said that the source of wealth is intellect, especially practical intellect, inventive and creative intellect. How should a society go about multiplying the activities of practical intellect? Intuitively, most people will want to say that development will occur best if very brilliant people sit down and make a plan for it. In this way, it seems at first, they can best create a rational design, so that all efforts will be bent to a single purpose, and so that little will be wasted or lost. In reality, however, this approach sometimes works; most often, it does not. And this high-frequency failure is for a systemic reason. Economic tasks are so complex, and depend upon the satisfaction of the ideals, wants, and desires of so many diverse citizens, that to limit creative intelligence to the small elite of rational planners is to impoverish the entire community. In practice, one achieves a greater critical mass of intelligence by actually multiplying the number of inventive and creative intellects who make their own choices. This method seems, at first, counterintuitive, but in practice it does seem to work best.

This decision is not made by ideology. It derives from a practical judgment, concerned about probable consequences. Practically speaking, an economic system seems to work best on a counterintuitive principle: not by rational command but, rather, only if one allows as much liberty as possible to every actor in the economic process, and thus multiplies the number of originating agents of insight and choice. Some such reasoning, for example, lay behind the Homestead Act in the United States, which multiplied the number of economic activists and property owners in the American West. Marx speaks somewhere of the "idiocy" of rural life. Such a characterization is no doubt too harsh in any environment, but it may refer to the passive attitudes of peasants who work entirely for a landed aristocracy, and have few if any rights of initiative on their own. It certainly does not characterize the multitude of independent farmers of the Middle West of the United States, each working as intelligently and creatively as possible, amazing in their capacity for practical invention, for improvisation, and for immense productivity.

The "land grant colleges" further institutionalized the American conviction that the source of wealth lies in the human intellect. These state universities were intended to develop new research and new methods, to be carried to every rural neighborhood through the statewide extension services. Finally, the state had further roles to play in the development of the North American West through the building of dams, the Highway Act, the Rural Electrification Act, farm credit, farm price supports, and in many other ways.

It is wrong to think that the system of democratic capitalism is a system of laissez-faire or free enterprise alone. On the contrary, the political system plays a role every bit as legitimate and every bit as necessary as that of the economic system. In democratic capitalist theory, the state is an *active* state. It is a major task of government "to promote the general welfare." As Madison saw, the state must promote the diversity of commerce and industry. Alexander Hamilton's work on the national bank, and on the banking system generally, and his *Report on Manufactures* also belong to the working practice of the political economy of democratic capitalism.

When we discuss "democracy and development," therefore, we find ourselves confronting two sets of problems. First, we must create the sorts of political institutions which make democracy real, and especially the actual observance of the human rights of all. Secondly, and just as urgently, we face the problem of creating economic institutions, and precisely those sorts of economic institutions which actually produce results. Every developing nation must produce sufficient new wealth to meet the growing expectations of its people. In thinking about political economy, therefore, it is necessary to think carefully about both poles of that expression: both about the institutions of the polity and about the institutions of the economy. Furthermore, both of these sets of institutions must be constantly criticized in the light of certain moral principles and of the human spirit. For it is the purpose of political economy to serve the development of human beings. And human beings are not solely political animals, or solely economic animals, but also, so to speak, inspirited animals, moral beings, children of God.

We come, then, not to two sets of institutional problems but to three. We want to create democracy. We also wish to effect development. Both of these tasks, to be accomplished well, make tremendous demands upon the social virtue and the human spirit of all citizens. Democracy and development are also, then, moral and spiritual tasks. They require healthy institutions of culture, education, the press, and religion.

Toward a Theology of Democracy and Development

While recent popes have begun to speak more and more frequently about the moral imperative of development, there is not yet a great deal of theological writing, particularly practical theological writing, about how such an imperative may actually be fulfilled. Suppose that

an entire people wished to produce both democracy and development. What ought they to do? What qualities of the human
spirit should they emphasize and nourish? For it is inconceivable that
one might produce democracy and development from just any spiritual premise at all. If, for example, individuals are not able to govern
themselves, how can they create self government in the polity? If
individuals are not able to deny themselves pleasures today, in order
to save and to invest for tomorrow, how then will they be able to
produce new wealth in the nation as a whole? If a people do not
develop habits of initiative, creative imagination, and invention in
their personal lives, then how will the society as a whole manifest a
creative dynamism? A practical theology of development depends
upon a practical pastoral theology, which will nourish effective habits
both in individuals and through specific institutions.

In the Catholic tradition since at least Leo XIII, we have a habit of
speaking of *social justice.* This is an important concept. It indicates that
justice is not solely a matter of the ethics of individual and family life,
but also of the workings of social institutions. Frequently, too, appeals
are made to *charity.* Yet it is remarkable how little thought we have
actually given to the virtues of development, the virtues of democracy, and the virtues of a political economy of pluralistic cultures. The
habits and dispositions for living well in such a world are surely
different in practice from those of the world before democracy, before
development, before pluralism. When development was not even a
dream, let alone a possibility, for example, one necessarily taught
oneself the virtues of *pazienza,* reconciliation, resignation, and even
obedience. When the will of God, however, seems rather suddenly to
call for development, quite new virtues are clearly called for—not
pazienza but inquiry, not fatalism but a search for practical measures of
improvement, not resignation but imagination and self-reliance, not
obedience only but the acceptance of one's own responsibilities for
action. We need, in a word, to think again about the *virtues* without
which democracy, development, and pluralism are not practicable.

I am by no means ready to answer fully the question I am here
raising. But at least this much is clear. There are two different ways of
thinking about virtue that will both need to be developed more fully.
The first way of thinking is classical. Just as Aristotle described from
acute observation of life around him in Athens the virtues held dear
by Athenians, so also we must imagine the virtues which are dear to
those who cherish democracy, development, and pluralism. This way
of thinking leads to virtues in the classical sense of dispositions and
habits of the individual person.

The second way of thinking is a little more difficult to conceptualize, but it corresponds to the general intention signified by the phrase *social justice*. It points less to the habits of individual persons than to the *institutions* which both depend upon and engender habits in individuals.

Let me employ what may at first seem like trifling examples: the institutions of baseball and soccer—each of which teaches virtues useful to development.

Baseball has several important characteristics. It is played by an *association*, whose success depends on each player. It celebrates the *individual*, each of whom is singled out by every movement of the ball, and each of whom, as batsman, must match wits and courage against the pitcher. It celebrates *law*, since every contingency is lovingly regulated by rules and every single play requires legitimation by an officer of the law, an umpire. It celebrates *wit*, since size and power are not decisive. It celebrates *checks and balances,* since every distance, height, weight, and length is calculated with concern for proportion and percentages.

Soccer, by contrast, is a game played by a collective, full of dash and *figura*. Although collective strategy, tactics, and team assistance are fundamental, each individual is free to play with *brio* and individual flair. Although law is present, it is scarcely obtrusive, and players can do whatever they can get away with. It teaches self-denial and patience, but also the quick seizing of sudden opportunities. It is in this way like investment. It demands great self-discipline and an instinct for the actions of others; it is in this way like corporate life. A little less admirably, but like American basketball, it also teaches a knack for feint and deception, and the ability to take swift advantage of the errors of others; it is an intense matching of wits rather than of brute strength. Soccer resembles in some of these ways North American basketball and in others North American football. It is gaining in popularity in the United States.

The two games teach admirable qualities, but not the same ones.

What is true of baseball and soccer is true of other institutions. We must ask which specific social virtues are required for and nurtured within educational systems of various sorts, in armies of various sorts, in business corporations of various sorts, in ecclesiastical institutions of various sorts, and in every other sort of institution. Clearly democratic institutions depend upon and nurture virtues different from those of classic authoritarian regimes. Institutions are social forms. They inculcate certain practices and attitudes.

If we are ever to have an adequate theology of the world, a

theology of the laity, and a theology of work, we must have a detailed taxonomy of the virtues which inform and are informed by the major institutions of modern life.

In closing, then, I would like to make at least a few tentative remarks about some of the virtues required by and inculcated through those economic institutions which create new wealth, the *institutions of development.* This list is not complete; and my remarks are mainly exploratory.

(1) *Stewardship.* It is Christian to recognize that the goods of the earth belong to all, and that those which come to owners of private property carry with them responsibilities for all. It is wrong to imagine that democratic capitalism demands laissez-faire, indifference to the lot of others, or self-centered consumption. Those who practice such vices poison the soil of the system they depend upon. For such a system is a social achievement; planted in barren land, property rights will speedily wither. The soil of a system of property rights depends upon the exercise of vigilant stewardship, so that the poorest and those in need are enabled to enter into its benefits and to contribute to its activities. If such a system is to win the loyalties of all, it must fairly reward the efforts of all, stimulate their talents, and promise and deliver opportunities to better their lot. Government must usually play a role in such stewardship, lending the weight of law to concern for the poor and needy. There are many debates about which methods best achieve results. Those societies in which all citizens become economic activists, however poor their origins, greatly multiply the sources of social intelligence.

(2) *The alleviation of poverty.* In a society aspiring to be just, several criteria must be met. (i) From decade to decade, the absolute and relative numbers of the poor ought to decrease. (ii) From decade to decade, the standard of what counts as poverty ought to rise. (iii) Institutions must be permeable and show such social fluidity that individuals, once in poorer categories, will rise into higher categories, and individuals once in higher categories will fall into lower ones. There should be some upward mobility, and some downward. (iv) All the poorest without exception should have a realistic hope of bettering their own lot during their lifetime. (v) Those unable to care for themselves must receive help.

(3) *Sacrifice for the future.* In order to produce new wealth for the future, citizens must set aside at least a small percentage of their present wealth, for *savings* and *investment.* Such virtue is indispensable. Obviously, it is less burdensome for those who live above subsistence levels. On the other hand, those who earn more must invest

more. The wealthy, in particular, must be encouraged to save and to invest, rather than merely to consume. In a purely hedonistic society, in which citizens live solely for the moment, the disciplines of a growth economy cannot be met. In traditional societies, the wealthy frequently squander their wealth in conspicuous consumption. Saved and invested in productive industries and commercial enterprises, by contrast, their wealth is put to social use. This is true even if, in so doing, their wealth remains in their own ownership and even if it grows. What is most decisive is that local wealth be withdrawn from consumption and be invested in providing goods and services of great social utility to others. Such investment stimulates invention, provides employment, and multiplies available goods and services. The virtues of investment must be taught.

(4) *Creativity and invention.* God bestows rare talents without regard to social category, so that a just society ought so to arrange its institutions as constantly to draw out from them the hidden talents and gifts dispersed even among the poorest and most humble. For often the greatest musicians and writers, mathematicians and generals, inventors and creators of enterprises are among those born poor. In *The American Challenge,* the French author Servan-Schreiber points out that the secret to the invention of new wealth is a society organized to find and to nourish creative talents wherever they may be found. And economists concerned with international economic development are coming more and more to stress the decisive importance of "human capital": that is, what goes on in the minds and spirits of citizens.

(5) *Associative skills.* Human beings are social animals, but in a different way from all other animals. For, while each has unique dignity and personhood, a sort of autonomy before God, they are, properly, neither individualists nor collectivists. When theologians write about "community," they tend to employ images derived from the village life of the medieval era and the modern small town or rural village. Yet there is a new form of community available and often practiced in modern societies: the community of voluntary association. In such associations, of many varied forms, individuals join together to accomplish common tasks or to seek common purposes. Typically, an individual belongs to many such associations, while belonging totally to none. In this sense, each lives a full and complex social life, not a lonely life. Yet no one association provides his or her total community. In such associations, especially when they are varied and multiple, each learns a wide range of social skills. In such a world, we do not bring up our children to be "rugged individualists,"

but to enjoy meeting others, to delight in habits of cooperation and dissent, to take pleasure in taking initiative and in experimenting in new ranges of human endeavor. The assumption is that each individual is complex and many-sided, and properly discovers in many different associations new dimensions of self-realization and fresh dimensions of sympathy. Sympathy, fellow-feeling, benevolence, tolerance, civil disagreement, a sense of fair play, a spirit of compromise and other-regardingness are taught in such associations. In them is developed what might be called "the pluralistic personality" or the "communitarian personality"—a distinctive modern type.

(6) *Entrepreneurial and commercial skills.* Classical philosophy regarded the merchant as a sub-moral type, and classical writers who praised the liberal arts often did so at the expense of the commercial arts and the industrial arts. In classical times, leisure was considered a high achievement. Today it is called unemployment. And, in most modern economies, the chief creator of new jobs is the small business sector. Thus anyone who sees unemployment as a moral problem— and in its effect upon family life, self-reliance, and independence of spirit, it is clearly a moral problem—must do everything possible to promote the multiplication of small businesses. This means high praise for the creators of new enterprises. This means praise for thrift and savings, for investment and risk taking, for honest accounting, for courteous service, for concern for the tastes, desires and needs expressed by the changing market, and for an entire range of human skills which measure the distance between success and failure. Those who create businesses serve the public, create employment, and enrich the public wealth by every increment of new wealth which they produce. Moreover, in contemporary industry, workers everywhere can work on exactly the same type of machines. What makes the difference is attention to quality—and quality is a fruit of the human spirit, not of machines. "Made in Chile" assesses the spirit with which Chilean workers accomplish their work: their pride, their attention, their sense for value and craftsmanship. The virtues of commerce and industry *are* virtues of the human spirit.

Conclusion

The creation of democracy and the achievement of development, in a word, depend on building institutions which engender such virtues as these, and which discourage their opposite vices. To be complete, one would also have to study the range of personal virtues, taught more properly in the family, in neighborhoods, in churches, and in schools, which are also required among peoples who aspire to achieve both democracy and development. I must be content, however, if I have said enough to justify the saying of Charles Péguy, one of my favorites: "The revolution is moral or not at all." A revolution of the human spirit is required to make both democracy and development living realities. That is reason enough for a poor theologian to be concerned with such this-worldly subjects.

This is the second lecture Michael Novak gave at the Pontifical University, Santiago, Chile, May 3–5, 1983. Reprinted from *Catholicism in Crisis*, October 1983.